PROBLEM SOLVING
for Teens™

An Interactive Approach
to Real-Life Problem Solving

Barbara J. Gray

LinguiSystems®

Problem/Skill Area:	Thinking
Developmental Age:	12 thru 18 years
Interest Level:	7th thru 12th grade
Reading Level:	2.5 — 3.5

LinguiSystems, Inc.
3100 4th Avenue
P.O. Box 747
East Moline, IL 61244

T 42784

1-800-PRO IDEA

ISBN 1-55999-113-5

About the Author

Barbara Gray, M.A., CCC is a speech-language pathologist for Township High School District #211 in Palatine, Illinois. She has worked with adolescents with communication disorders for eight years, including those with learning disabilities, developmental handicaps, physical handicaps, and those learning English as a second language.   She has also worked with regular education students. In addition to working in the school district, Barbara maintains a private practice and enjoys her two young children at home.   *Problem Solving for Teens* is Barbara's first publication with LinguiSystems.

August 1990

Dedication

To my husband, Randy, and my children, Chelsea and Alyssa, whose support, suggestions, and distractions were crucial in creating *Problem Solving for Teens*

I also want to thank my students for helping me develop and test the problem-solving process presented in this book.

Finally, I would like to thank Aliceann Sanders, who will be missed in her retirement, but whose wisdom I will always value.

We welcome your comments on *Problem Solving for Teens* and other LinguiSystems products.   Please send your comments to:

Carolyn Blagden
Editorial Manager
LinguiSystems, Inc.
3100 4th Avenue
P.O. Box 747
East Moline, IL 61244

TABLE OF CONTENTS

INTRODUCTION

Teenaged students are faced with problems every day. Good problem-solving skills are crucial to their survival. As your students venture into adolescence, they have an increased responsibility to make choices in their ever-changing world. Unfortunately, many students with language or learning disabilities don't develop good problem-solving skills on their own. They need direct instruction to learn how to solve problems in a logical manner. They also need "safe" practice situations during which they can gain the confidence they need for solving problems independently in their own lives. *Problem Solving for Teens* offers your students a step-by-step process for problem solving, encouraging them to build independent thinking and problem-solving skills.

Each unit begins with a goal and a list of objectives related to a step of problem solving. Next, teaching suggestions are provided to address these objectives and give you background information to discuss with your students before they do the worksheets. Then, worksheets and additional activities are provided for each objective. The worksheets can be reproduced and given to your students to work on individually or in groups. Use the worksheets as discussion starters for further exploration of the problem-solving step or of a particular problem situation. Encourage your students to share their experiences as you discuss and practice the problem-solving steps. No answer key is needed because there are many acceptable responses. The additional activities are designed to reinforce what your students have learned and to show them how to carry over those skills to their daily lives.

These activities are suitable for groups or individuals. Group interaction frequently results in students modeling appropriate problem-solving strategies for each other, encouraging students to learn from one another. The worksheets offer you more freedom to work with individuals, encourage independent attempts at problem solving, and give your students opportunities to work at their own pace.

The appendix includes one review sheet for each unit. These review sheets are flexible, allowing you to fill in as much information as you want, and have your students fill in the rest. Your students can use these review sheets to practice the crucial elements of each problem-solving step. In addition to the review sheets, there are three pages which list typical problem situations encountered by teenagers. You can use these pages as a reference to make up problem situations for your students to solve.

The real-life situations your students find in *Problem Solving for Teens* will spur them on to better problem solving. As they identify with the problems, your students will be motivated to develop their problem-solving skills and use them in their own surroundings, whether they're at home, at school, at work, or with their friends. They'll soon be taking the initiative to solve their own problems in an organized, efficient way!

Barbara

PROBLEMS

Goal: To identify, classify and explain problems.

OBJECTIVES

IDENTIFYING PROBLEMS: To learn and apply the criteria for identifying a problem.

CATEGORIZING PROBLEMS: To categorize problems by difficulty to solve. To prioritize problems by severity and urgency.

RECOGNIZING SIGNS: To recognize clues like facial expressions and body language to identify problems.

DETERMINING RESPONSIBILITY: To determine who's responsible for solving a problem.

This section of *Problem Solving for Teens* contains exercises for your students to practice identifying and classifying problems in their everyday lives. The exercises will help them recognize why these problems occur and their responsibility for solving them. Through follow-up discussions, you can also increase your students' awareness of individual problem solving styles and how each style reflects a judgment based on what is important to each person.

TEACHING SUGGESTIONS

1. Before each exercise, review the definition of a problem: a problem is a situation which needs to be fixed or changed. Next, provide a situation to discuss. Have your students decide if a problem is present. Then, talk about the different opinions that result from individual problem solving styles and personal values. Encourage your students to accept that what may be a problem for one person may not be a problem for another.

2. When you talk about clues that signal problems, let your students first identify the concrete visual or auditory warning signs given off by machines and inanimate objects. Ask them to describe what machines do to signal a problem. Discuss small clues that signal trouble early on and then differentiate them from more serious signs. Use common items like a rug, a vacuum, a toaster, a cassette tape player, or a car. Then, let your students apply their knowledge to the physical signs a baby might give when in distress, or what aches in their own bodies might mean. Point out that almost everything gives warning signs of distress.

   Have your students observe facial expressions and body language as they encounter situations with their friends and families. Tell them to notice how people act when they're upset. Explain that the way someone holds his head, how he looks or makes eye contact, how he speaks, and how he acts when nervous are all clues that might signal a problem. Encourage your students to record their observations and then share them with the class.

3. Help your students learn to recognize signs of problems by increasing their sensitivity to their surroundings and to other people. Use one of these exercises for practice:

   ❑ Make a tape of noises from a variety of settings. Then, ask your students to identify the noises.

   ❑ Use photographs or magazine pictures to have your students practice identifying signs of problems through facial expressions.

   ❑ Take photographs of your students or have students volunteer to take photographs of people exhibiting facial expressions that signal problems. Or, let your students role-play situations to portray a variety of clues. Photograph or videotape them as they role-play.

4. Help your students increase their awareness of responsibility for solving problems by discussing their responsibilities at home. Also involve your students' parents by sending home a questionnaire to survey your students' home responsibilities. Encourage parents to have their son or daughter help at home to practice responsibility.

5. Begin a discussion of who's responsible for solving problems by presenting examples from your own life or from television and books. Ask your students to volunteer their own examples, if possible, and focus primarily on their successes in problem solving. Help them realize that the person who causes a problem is generally responsible for its solution.

6. Any time you provide sample situations for discussion, include an example related to home, work, school, or personal relationships. Providing a variety of relevant examples will help your students draw the connection between problem solving practice and their own lives. It also ensures that students will be able to relate to some of the experiences described.

Yes or No?

Is every situation you face a problem? Read each situation below. Decide if it would be a problem for you by circling **Yes**, **No**, or **Could Be**.

Then, use the line below each situation to explain your choice. Keep in mind that what may be a problem for one person may not be a problem for someone else.

Example:

You arrived at school early.   Yes   No   (Could Be)

I might not be able to get in because the doors may still be locked.

1. Your pet ran away.   Yes   No   Could Be

   _____

2. You can't find your other shoe.   Yes   No   Could Be

   _____

3. Your best friend skipped school today.   Yes   No   Could Be

   _____

4. You got a B on the spelling test.   Yes   No   Could Be

   _____

5. You fell asleep at 9:00 P.M.   Yes   No   Could Be

   _____

6. Your boss raised your wages.   Yes   No   Could Be

   _____

7. You missed your ride.   Yes   No   Could Be

   _____

8. Your teacher wants you to stay after class. Yes   No   Could Be

   _____

Day to Day

Would these situations be problems for you?
Read each situation below. Decide if the
situation would be a problem for you and write
Yes or **No** on the blank.

Then, use the line below each situation to
explain your choice.

Example:

_No_____   You forgot your pencil.

I can borrow one from the teacher. _____

1. _____   You can't get your locker open.

    _____

2. _____   You have a half day of school today.

    _____

3. _____   You want a candy bar.

    _____

4. _____   Your sister borrowed your cassette tape.

    _____

5. _____   They're serving pizza in the cafeteria.

    _____

6. _____   You forgot to eat dinner before you went to work.

    _____

7. _____   Your parents are out of town this weekend.

    _____

8. _____   You sit in the back row of math class.

    _____

10

It's Your Choice

You decide when a situation is a problem. Read each situation below. Then, write **P** on the blank if it's a problem or **NP** if it's not a problem.

1. _____ You drop your books in the hallway on the way to your next class. Other students walking by don't seem to notice.

2. _____ You have a ten o'clock curfew on school nights. Your best friend can stay out as late as he wants. Tonight is a school night and both of you are going to an away basketball game that won't be over before 9:30.

3. _____ A friend loans you several music cassette tapes. You listen to them all night.

4. _____ Your brother has been watching TV alone for over two hours. Now you want to watch a show but he has the channel selector.

5. _____ Your allowance is six dollars a week. You plan to go to a movie that will cost you three dollars plus the cost of popcorn.

6. _____ You're in a record store with a friend. You see her shoplift a cassette tape. When you tell her to put it back, she laughs at you.

7. _____ You forgot your lunch money again. No one will loan you any money.

8. _____ You left your book for history class at home. Your teacher has told you to bring the book to class every day. Today you need it for an assignment.

9. _____ Your boss insists that you work overtime tonight. It's now nine o'clock and your parents won't let you work after nine o'clock.

10. _____ Your coat zipper won't work. It's warm outside and you have to walk home.

Detective Work

You can tell when there's a problem by looking for clues. Read each situation below. Look for problem clues. Then, describe the problem on the line below each situation.

Example:

Doug borrowed $20 from his brother on Tuesday. He promised to repay the money within a week. On Wednesday, Doug found out he lost his job.

What's the problem?   *Doug might not have the money to repay his brother in time*

because he's not working this week.

1. Jackie spent six hours in the sun on the first day of her vacation. Now, her back hurts and her eyes are swollen.

   What's the problem? _____

   _____

2. Stan's teacher says he didn't return a book that he checked out. He doesn't know where to find the book.

   What's the problem? _____

   _____

3. Kathy drove her mom's car without asking. She hit another car in a parking lot and put a big dent in it. No one was in the other car.

   What's the problem? _____

   _____

4. Tammy got an *F* on her science test. She has already failed two tests in science class and her parents grounded her. Tammy thinks she studies very hard for her science class.

   What's the problem? _____

   _____

5. Ann and Sarah sat together in the cafeteria. Other students teased Sarah about her weight. Sarah ran out the door crying. She left all her books in the cafeteria.

   What's the problem? _____

   _____

Fix It or Leave It

You know there's a problem if you need to fix something about it. Read each situation below. Underline the situation if you think it's a problem. Then, use the line below the problem to explain why it's a problem.

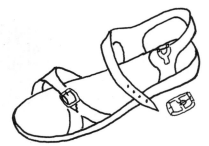

Example:

<u>You bought a new pair of sandals and a buckle is broken.</u>

It's the only pair of summer shoes I have. _____

1. You fell asleep while you were doing homework for tomorrow.

   _____

2. Your sister says she doesn't like her English teacher.

   _____

3. Your English teacher has scheduled a test for Friday.

   _____

4. You just found out you have to work on Christmas Eve.

   _____

5. The telephone in the living room doesn't work.

   _____

6. You tripped over a rock in the parking lot and skinned your knee.

   _____

7. You made the basketball team.

   _____

8. Your best friend is moving to another state.

   _____

9. Your parents let you use the car tonight to go to the school dance.

   _____

10. You need to buy a book for school tomorrow, but you've already spent your weekly allowance.

    _____

Explain Why

There's often more than one reason for a problem. Read each situation below. Then, write two reasons it could be a problem.

Example:

   Situation: You lost your watch.

   Why could it be a problem?   _It was my grandfather's watch and it was worth $200._

1.   Situation: You flunked your final English test.

     Why could it be a problem?   _____

     _____

2.   Situation: You forgot to give your dad a phone message.

     Why could it be a problem?   _____

     _____

3.   Situation: You ripped a huge hole in a pair of pants.

     Why could it be a problem?   _____

     _____

4.   Situation: Your friend was suspended from school.

     Why could it be a problem?   _____

     _____

5.   Situation: You talked back to your mother today.

     Why could it be a problem?   _____

     _____

14

ADDITIONAL ACTIVITIES

Students need a variety of experiences to help them practice identifying problems. Use the activities below to help your students better identify situations in their own lives that might be potential problems.

❑ Bring in several magazines featuring people in everyday situations. Have each student choose a scene from a magazine and list five possible problems suggested by the picture. Then, have each student exchange the picture with another student and list five more problems of his own for the new picture. Later, have each pair of students discuss their lists of problems and compare their opinions.

❑ Provide a variety of media from which your students can identify potential problems. Using magazines, videotapes, filmstrips, written stories, personal experience, or personal observation, have your students identify potential problems.

Divide your students into pairs. Have one student use the media to identify a situation. Ask the second student to decide if a situation is a problem. If the student identifies the situation as a problem, he then tells why.

Later, have your students write a brief description of each situation and their opinions about each situation. Finally, have your students share the situations and their opinions with the rest of the class.

❑ Encourage your students to observe possible problem situations in their own homes. Design a simple recording form for your students to record information about the problems. Have them answer questions like *What problem did you notice? Who was involved in the problem? Were the same people always involved? Will any of the problems get worse?*

❑ Have your students write five to ten situations that occur at home, and five to ten situations that occur at school. Then, have them share the situations in pairs. Have each student decide if a situation is a problem. Next, have each pair of students compare their opinions. Later, have your students share their situations and opinions with the rest of the class.

Easy or Hard?

Life is full of problems. Some of them are more serious than others and harder to fix.

Read each problem below. Next, decide how serious it is by circling the words **Easy to Fix** or **Hard to Fix.** Then, explain your choice.

Example:

You have a toothache.   Easy to Fix   (Hard to Fix)

I'll have to see the dentist.   That will take time and money. _____

1. Your pencil lead broke.   Easy to Fix   Hard to Fix

    _____

2. You lost your wallet.   Easy to Fix   Hard to Fix

    _____

3. You have food stuck between your teeth.   Easy to Fix   Hard to Fix

    _____

4. You were caught shoplifting.   Easy to Fix   Hard to Fix

    _____

5. Your school bus was five minutes late.   Easy to Fix   Hard to Fix

    _____

6. Your hair is a mess.   Easy to Fix   Hard to Fix

    _____

7. It's raining outside.   Easy to Fix   Hard to Fix

    _____

8. Your bike tire is low on air.   Easy to Fix   Hard to Fix

    _____

9. You're sick and you didn't call in to work.   Easy to Fix   Hard to Fix

    _____

10. You didn't finish your homework.   Easy to Fix   Hard to Fix

    _____

How Serious Is It?

Name _____

We face several problems every day, so we have to know which problems are the most serious. Read each problem below. Then, rate the seriousness of the problem by labeling it **Easy, Medium, or Hard to Fix**.

E	= Easy to Fix
M	= Medium to Fix
H	= Hard to Fix

1. _____ You spilled ketchup on a sweater you borrowed.

2. _____ You're sitting in math class and you notice your fly is unzipped.

3. _____ Your teacher caught you sleeping in class.

4. _____ You lost a glove.

5. _____ You were turned down for a date to a dance.

6. _____ Your tire is flat.

7. _____ You broke a lamp in the living room.

8. _____ You failed your science test.

9. _____ You lost the permission form to go on a class field trip.

10. _____ You left work early for an appointment but forgot to tell your boss.

11. _____ Your new sweater shrank when you put it in the dryer.

12. _____ You're addressing an envelope to your grandpa, but you don't know his ZIP Code.

13. _____ You have a math test tomorrow, but you left your notes at school.

14. _____ You're baking a cake when the electricity goes off for an hour.

Which problem above would be the hardest to solve? Why? _____

_____

17

Do It Now

What emergencies have you handled?
A problem can be an emergency if it
needs to be solved immediately.

Read each problem below. Next, write
the word **Now** or **Later** before each problem
to show when it should be solved. Then,
explain your choice.

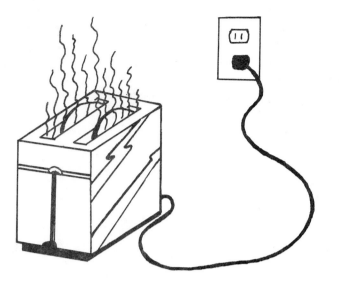

Example:

Now _____ The toaster is smoking and you smell something burning.

If I don't take care of it now, a fire may start. _____

1. _____ Your dresser drawers are getting very messy.

_____

2. _____ Your girlfriend thinks you lied to her about something.

_____

3. _____ Your dog made a mess on the carpeting. No one else is home.

_____

4. _____ You forgot to turn on the oven for your mom. She's pulling into the driveway.

_____

5. _____ Your little sister is begging you to take her to the park.

_____

6. _____ Your teacher thinks you were cheating on a test.

_____

7. _____ You haven't kept in touch with a friend who moved away.

_____

8. _____ You have a B in English. Your semester exams are in three weeks.

_____

18

Say When

Name _____

Have you ever solved a problem immediately because it might have gotten worse if you didn't?

Read each problem below. Then, decide when to solve the problem by circling the word **Now**, **Soon**, or **Later**. Remember that your opinions may be different from someone else's opinions.

1.	Your brother just fell off his bike. He's bleeding heavily from several cuts.	Now	Soon	Later
2.	You're in class and you feel like you might throw up.	Now	Soon	Later
3.	You need a physical to try out for basketball. Tryouts are in one week.	Now	Soon	Later
4.	Your bike tire needs air.	Now	Soon	Later
5.	You ripped the seat of your pants in class.	Now	Soon	Later
6.	The grass on your lawn is too long. It's your job to cut it.	Now	Soon	Later
7.	Your friend is in the hospital and he wants you to visit.	Now	Soon	Later
8.	Christmas is four months away and you haven't saved any money for gifts.	Now	Soon	Later
9.	A customer where you work is angry and wants to see your boss.	Now	Soon	Later
10.	You owe ten dollars on clothing you have on layaway. It's due in two weeks.	Now	Soon	Later
11.	Your grandparents are going to celebrate their 50th wedding anniversary next year, and you want to buy them a nice gift.	Now	Soon	Later
12.	You're taking notes and your pencil lead breaks.	Now	Soon	Later
13.	You need to return a shirt to a store because it doesn't fit.	Now	Soon	Later
14.	You dropped a glass and it broke.	Now	Soon	Later

It's Not My Day!

Everyone has "bad" days when nothing seems to go right. Read the sentences below that tell a story about one person's bad day.

Next, underline the sentences that describe a problem. Then, write **Now**, **Soon**, or **Later** on the blank to tell when to solve the problem.

Be careful — some sentences aren't problems!

1. _____ My alarm woke me up at 6:30.

2. _____ As I sat up to get out of bed, I hit the lamp next to my bed with my arm. The lamp went crashing to the floor.

3. _____ Next, I walked into the bathroom and took a nice, warm shower.

4. _____ As I got dressed, I looked around for my gym shoes but couldn't find them.

5. _____ After that, I went to the kitchen to eat.

6. _____ First, I burned my toast.

7. _____ Then, I spilled my glass of juice.

8. _____ Finally, I finished breakfast and made it to the bus on time.

9. _____ As I sat down in my bus seat, I remembered that I'd left my biology assignment on the kitchen table.

10. _____ When I got to school, I found out my friend was sick at home.

I hope I don't have a bad day like this every day!

ADDITIONAL ACTIVITIES

Two of the most difficult tasks in problem solving are identifying the severity of problems and setting priorities for solving them. Many students find it difficult to differentiate one problem from another, and consequently view all problems the same way. To help your students better identify the severity of a problem and prioritize the need for solving it, use the activities below.

❑ Provide each student with a list of ten problems. Have your students read the problems independently and rate them as *easy*, *medium*, or *hard* to fix. Next, have them look at the problems again and decide which problems need to be solved now and which problems can wait. Then, have them compare their opinions with another student. Later, hold a class discussion about the different problem solving styles they observed. For example, some of them may have found hard problems easier and quicker to solve than less serious problems.

❑ Tell your students to think through all the events they experienced prior to class. Have each of them list five problems they experienced themselves or observed that day. Next, have them rate the problems as *easy*, *medium*, or *hard* to fix. As an extra activity, have your students indicate if the problem was solved by writing *yes* or *no* after the problem. Later, discuss the problems with the class. Encourage them to notice what kinds of problems were easy, medium or hard to solve. Also, encourage them to notice people's different problem solving styles and how perspectives change depending on who you are and what you bring to a situation.

❑ Let your students practice prioritizing when problems should be solved by having them list three problems they'd solve right away and three problems they could solve later. Tell them to be able to explain the reasons behind their choices. Then, hold a class discussion and let your students share their lists of problems and how they would prioritize them.

Looking for Clues

What makes you decide to throw an object away or replace it with a new one? The clues you see or hear often tell you there's a problem.

Read each problem below. Then, list the problem clues you might see or hear.

Example:

Problem	Clues You See	Clues You Hear
An old cassette tape is wearing out.	*loose tape*	*muffled music*

Problem	Clues You See	Clues You Hear
1. Your desk light might go out.	_____	_____
2. It might storm.	_____	_____
3. Your jeans might rip.	_____	_____
4. Your bicycle tire is getting flat.	_____	_____
5. The cereal box is almost empty.	_____	_____
6. Your car needs a new muffler.	_____	_____
7. The door lock needs to be fixed.	_____	_____
8. Your pen is almost out of ink.	_____	_____
9. Food is overcooking on the stove.	_____	_____
10. You're getting a cold.	_____	_____
11. Your house needs to be painted.	_____	_____
12. The piano needs to be tuned.	_____	_____
13. The kitchen faucet is leaking.	_____	_____
14. Your shoe heel needs to be replaced.	_____	_____

22

Warning Signs

Sometimes you can fix a problem if you notice clues about it ahead of time.

Read the list of objects below. Then, write two clues that could signal a possible problem. Remember, what you hear and see are often good clues about the problem.

Example:

Object	Problem Clues
bike tire	a. *tire looks flat*
	b. *hissing sound is coming from tire*

Object	Problem Clues
1. toaster	a. _____
	b. _____
2. typewriter ribbon	a. _____
	b. _____
3. stereo speakers	a. _____
	b. _____
4. lawn mower	a. _____
	b. _____
5. pencil sharpener	a. _____
	b. _____
6. candy machine	a. _____
	b. _____
7. watch	a. _____
	b. _____
8. TV	a. _____
	b. _____

23

Open Your Eyes

People give clues about their problems. If you watch their facial expressions and actions closely, you can often tell what the problem is.

Read each problem below. Then, look at the clues inside the Clue Box and write the letters of the clues you might see. You can use a clue more than once.

Clue Box

A – pale looking	G – biting fingernails	L – pacing the floor
B – red faced	H – holding head in hand	M – looking down
C – eyes wide	I – stammers when speaking	N – eyes closed
D – crying	J – leaning back in chair	O – frown on face
E – tight lips	K – head lying in arms	P – fidgeting hands
F – tapping feet		

Clues   Problems

_____   1. You're home alone at night.

_____   2. Your older brother has been fired from his job.

_____   3. A student has been listening to a lecture for over a half hour.

_____   4. A girl ate a whole pizza, four candy bars, some cotton candy, and a bag of chips.

_____   5. Your little brother's dog is missing.

_____   6. A student can't spell a word.

_____   7. A little boy is caught lying.

_____   8. A speaker is waiting to make a speech.

_____   9. Your locker is stuck and you need your books.

Make up your own problem. Have someone else give the clues for the problem.

Clues   Problem

_____   10. _____

_____

People Watching

Name _____

People who are upset, angry or nervous often show it in how they look and what they do.

Read each story below. Decide how the person feels by noticing his facial expression and his actions. Next, circle the word below the story that describes his feelings. Then, use the line to explain what problem might have caused this feeling.

Example:

Betsy's mom walked to the window and looked out. She walked back and sat down in a chair. When a car drove by outside, she jumped up from her chair and looked out the window again.

What's this person feeling?   mad   sad   (nervous)   lonely

What could the problem be?   *Betsy's late getting home and hasn't called.*

1. Joe stared at the floor as he waited. He held a rolled up magazine and bounced it on his legs from time to time. Each time a door opened or someone spoke, he looked up from the floor and frowned.

    What's this person feeling?   mad   sad   nervous   lonely

    What could the problem be? _____

2. Ms. Brown glared at her class from the front of the room. She held a pile of papers in her hand. As she crossed her arms, she pressed her lips together as if to keep from saying something. Then, she walked towards her desk and threw the papers down.

    What's this person feeling?   mad   sad   nervous   lonely

    What could the problem be? _____

Now, make up a story yourself. Then, have someone else answer the questions.

Story: _____

_____

_____

_____

What's this person feeling?   mad   sad   nervous   lonely

What could the problem be? _____

ADDITIONAL ACTIVITIES

An important part of problem solving is being aware of events occuring around you and what they mean. Many students find it hard to focus on these events and the signs that indicate a possible problem. The activities below will help your students increase their awareness of potential problems.

❑ Have your students wear something unusual or do something different with their hair. To remind them, put a note on the door for them to see as they enter the room. If needed, have them change something quickly, like untucking a shirt or switching socks with another person. Then, have each student write down names and the differences they see. Later, let them compare notes to see who noticed the most changes. Follow the exercise with a discussion about the importance of being aware of clues about problem situations.

❑ Give your students practice using all of their senses to detect problems. Use items in your classroom to focus on the clues that objects give when they have problems. Hold up or point to an item and have your students volunteer clues about it. Have them think about what they might hear, see, feel, or smell that would indicate a problem.

Have your students bring in small objects or find pictures of objects. Then, tell them to make a written list of clues about the object that could signal problems. Discuss clues like warning lights, unusual sounds or smells, worn areas, slower operation, sparks, and smoke. Encourage each student to offer several clues for an object. Then, let your students share their objects and list of clues to see if there are other clues to notice.

❑ Using magazine pictures or photographs, have your students observe facial expressions and look for signs of potential problems. Then, let them exchange pictures or photographs and discuss their opinions.

Talk about basic emotion vocabulary words, like *nervous, mad, sad* or *lonely*. Discuss the facial expressions and body language associated with each word. Also, talk about auditory warnings, like a rise in voice volume or tapping sounds, that might show various emotions.

Bring in some reference books about body language. Give your students time to read them and talk about them, if they wish.

Play a game of charades. Have your students role-play situations using facial expressions and body language. Then, let the other students guess what the problems might be. Discuss the clues that led them to their decisions.

Whose Problem Is It?

Name _____

Do you think you should solve a problem caused by your younger brother or a friend? The person who caused the problem is usually the one who should fix it.

Read each problem below. Then, match the problem with the person who should solve it by writing the correct letter in the blank. You can use a letter more than once.

Problems

1. _____ Your sister might have the measles.

2. _____ You borrowed your neighbor's snow shovel, but now you can't find it.

3. _____ You didn't do your homework, and you have a quiz today.

4. _____ Your friend shot a golf ball through the neighbor's window.

5. _____ A baby fell off the bed and hit his head while your sister was babysitting.

6. _____ You burned the spaghetti.

7. _____ A customer ordered a cheeseburger, but you gave him a hamburger instead.

8. _____ Your dad ran over the bike your brother left in the driveway.

9. _____ Your neighbor ran over your cat and injured it.

10. _____ Your friend told you a secret. You told someone else. Now, your friend is mad.

11. _____ Your mom is taking care of a baby who has a dirty diaper.

12. _____ You loaned a book to your brother and he lost it.

13. _____ You broke your leg.

14. _____ Your dad spilled a glass of milk in the kitchen.

Solvers

a. your mom

b. your friend

c. the baby

d. your sister

e. the neighbor

f. your brother

g. your dad

h. the doctor

i. you

Determining Responsibility

27

Why Me?

Taking responsibility for your problems is an important step in successful problem solving.

Read each problem below. Then, explain why you should be the person responsible for solving the problem described.

Example:

Your room is messy. Why should you clean your own room? *I should clean my own*

room because I messed it up and I live there.

1. You broke your tape cassette player. Why should you pay for fixing it? _____

_____

2. You don't understand your homework assignment. Why should you talk to the teacher

about it? _____

_____

3. You drove 30 miles to see a movie. Why should you pay for the gas? _____

_____

4. You're late for track practice. Why should you explain why you're late? _____

_____

5. You made a long-distance phone call to a friend. Why should you pay for the call?

_____

6. You can't work when you're supposed to. Why should you find someone else to take your

place? _____

_____

7. You stayed in the hall talking to a friend, and now you're late for class.   Why should you

explain the reason you're late? _____

_____

8. You backed the family car into a telephone post and broke a tail light. Why should you

pay for a new tail light? _____

_____

Help, Please!

Sometimes problems are too hard to handle because you don't know how to solve them, or someone else can solve it better. That's when you need to ask for help.

Read each problem below. Then, decide if you'd need help by using the rating scale below. Remember that your opinions may be different from someone else's opinions.

A — I can solve it.
B — I need some help.
C — Someone else can solve it better.

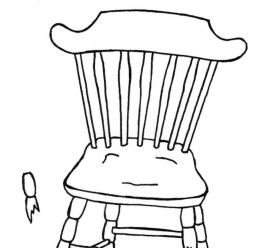

Example:

    C   You were goofing off and broke the leg on a chair.

    A   It's raining outside and you usually walk home.

1. _____ Your grandfather had a heart attack.

2. _____ You spilled milk on the table.

3. _____ You can't decide what audiotape to buy.

4. _____ You don't understand the directions to a friend's house.

5. _____ Your garage is on fire.

6. _____ You forgot your lunch money.

7. _____ You were caught off school grounds when you should have been in class.

8. _____ The little boy you were babysitting fell and cut his knee badly.

9. _____ You got a speeding ticket while driving your father's car.

10. _____ You were late to meet a friend at the library, and now he's gone.

11. _____ The bathroom sink is clogged.

12. _____ You don't understand a difficult math problem.

13. _____ The washing machine won't fill up with water.

14. _____ You need a hanger to hang up your coat.

       29

Who's in Charge?

Taking responsibilty for a problem means being responsible for solving it. It also means knowing when to ask someone else for help.

Read each problem below. First, decide who should solve it. Then, decide if you need someone to help you. Write your answers in the correct blanks. Remember that your opinions may be different from someone else's opinions.

Example:

The little boy you're babysitting is being hit by his friend.

Solver   _the babysitter_   Helper   _the friend's mother_

1. You and a friend were riding bikes when he ran into you. Your bike is wrecked.

   Solver _____   Helper _____

2. You didn't finish your homework because your brother got hurt and went to the hospital. You went with him.

   Solver _____   Helper _____

3. You want to ask a girl for a date. You're shy, but your friend, Dan, is a talker. You haven't talked to this girl very much, but you know some of her friends.

   Solver _____   Helper _____

4. Your boss asked you to do a job you've never done before.

   Solver _____   Helper _____

5. You borrowed your mother's car and left the headlights on. Now, the battery is dead.

   Solver _____   Helper _____

6. You were playing baseball in the street when your friend hit the ball through a neighbor's window.

   Solver _____   Helper _____

7. You need a shirt ironed for a music concert and you're the only one home.

   Solver _____   Helper _____

8. You checked several books out of the library. You loaned one of them to a friend, and he lost it.

   Solver _____   Helper _____

Determining Responsibility   30   Copyright © 1990 LinguiSystems, Inc.

Initiating the problem solving process requires a decision about who's responsible for solving the problem. For some students, assuming responsibilty is a difficult task because it means putting forth effort towards a solution, or admitting a need for help. Use the activities below to help your students practice assuming responsibility.

❑ Use examples of typical classroom problems to focus on taking responsibility for solutions. If possible, allow your students to volunteer their own examples of problems. When examples are provided, discuss the problems and who caused them. Remind them that the person who caused the problem is usually responsible for solving it.

Encourage your students to decide when to seek help with a solution for problems that are too hard or serious to solve or that require special information that they don't have. Examine the effects of some solutions, particularly those which have been positive. Look at solutions with negative effects as opportunities to reexamine the solutions that were used and to look for alternatives.

❑ Discuss problems relating to classroom materials, noise or sight distractions, listening difficulties, and care of belongings. Share examples of problems you've had, too, if you wish.

❑ Have your students volunteer their own problems. Lead them through the problem solving steps they've learned by asking questions like *Who caused the problem? What exactly was the problem? Who solved the problem? Should the person have asked for help? Who else should have solved the problem?* Discuss problems that were solved with both effective and ineffective solutions. Encourage your students to examine why the solution worked out as it did and who should or could have solved it.

❑ To help your students assume responsibility, give them opportunities to take charge in the classroom. Have them do things like clean up activities, organize desks, gather papers, or help others with a learning task. Later. hold a class discussion to talk about how your students felt when they took responsibility.

CHOICES

Goal: To generate and evaluate possible solutions.

OBJECTIVES

CHOOSING REACTIONS: To recognize the difference between a quick reaction and a controlled reaction to a problem.

GENERATING SOLUTIONS: To generate multiple solutions to a problem.

ASSESSING RESOURCES: To assess a need for help and then evaluate possible resources.

EVALUATING SOLUTIONS: To weigh the advantages and disadvantages of a given solution.

This section of *Problem Solving for Teens* contains exercises for your students to practice making choices in a planned and organized manner.   The exercises will help them recognize the importance of making independent decisions, while realistically examining their options and resources.   Through follow-up discussions, you can also increase your students' understanding of the reflective nature of problem solving.

TEACHING SUGGESTIONS

1.   Before beginning the exercises, review the process for identifying and explaining problems.   Reproduce the flow chart below or make a transparency to remind your students that this is only the first step of the five-step problem solving process. Give your students a brief overview of each step to help them understand what's involved in each one.

PROBLEM

↓

CHOICES

↓

PLANS

↓

RESULTS

↓

PREVENTING PROBLEMS

2.   Hold a class discussion to talk about problem solving styles and the need to approach a problem with control.   Compare solving a problem quickly and emotionally versus thinking through solutions and potential outcomes.   Give your students examples of typical problems, especially classroom-related ones, that were solved impulsively and discuss their outcomes.

3. Teach your students these new words related to planned problem solving. Discuss them and provide examples for illustration.

   Assertive means having a positive or "I can do it" attitude. People who handle a problem assertively show their positive attitude through their facial expressions and body language.

   Independent means trying to handle problems on your own. Independence doesn't mean having to do it all by yourself. Many times, being independent is knowing where to go for help and then asking for it.

   Reflective means thinking through all of your choices. Most problems are not emergencies, so there's time to examine a problem thoroughly to choose the best solution.

   Next, have your students role-play some situations to make sure they understand these words. Ask questions like:

   > *How would you act assertively in this situation?*
   > *How could you handle this problem independently?*
   > *What do you need to do to examine all the choices?*
   > *What would be a quick or emotional reaction to this problem?*
   > *How did the solution work out?*

4. To encourage your students to generate multiple solutions, suggest that they write down any solution they can think of, good or bad. Tell them to think of all the resources they could use to solve a problem, even if it sounds silly at this point. Remind them that effective solutions often come from imaginative suggestions.

   Let your students work in pairs to learn the benefit of teamwork in generating ideas.

5. Help your students develop a healthy attitude towards asking questions by providing opportunities to ask and accept questions. Give them representative problems where they need to ask for help. Encourage your students to focus on what's needed to solve a problem. Discuss the value of questioning and what happens if questions are not asked.

   Talk about "safe" times and "safe" people to question. Discuss asking a teacher questions after class or catching a friend or parent when he isn't busy.

6. As your students explore solution options, remind them that there are consequences to their actions. Teach them to predict outcomes by asking *What would happen if?* questions.

   If a solution can cause harm or has a great cost attached to it, advise your students to examine another option. Cost can be in the form of money, embarrassment, loss of friendship, physical harm, or a serious misunderstanding.

   Have your students explore the possibility of new problems arising from a particular solution. Provide examples of simple and complex problems and have your students brainstorm new problems that could arise.

Try It

Solving a problem too quickly can sometimes cause you trouble. Take the time to think about every possible solution before you react.

Read each problem below. Write a letter **T** in the blank if it's a reaction showing thinking. Write a letter **Q** if the reaction is too quick.

Example:

Someone calls you a name in class.

Q   You hit him.

T   You ignore him.

1. Your parents won't let you have the car for two weeks.

    _____ a.   You discuss it with them and explain how you've helped more lately.

    _____ b.   You shout at them and pound the wall.

2. Someone you don't know shoves you at a party.

    _____ a.   You shove him back.

    _____ b.   You take a step back and turn to leave the room.

3. You're talking to a friend on the phone and your dad tells you to get off the phone.

    _____ a.   You tell him "I'm not finished yet" and keep on talking.

    _____ b.   You tell your friend you have to get off the phone and say good-bye.

4. Your teacher returns an assignment to you and tells you to redo it.

    _____ a.   You ask her when it needs to be done and then put the assignment away.

    _____ b.   You wad the paper up and throw it angrily into the wastebasket.

5. Your sister gives you back a sweater she borrowed. The sweater is dirty.

    _____ a.   You remind her that she needs to return the clothes clean so you can wear them.

    _____ b.   You shout at her and tell her she can't borrow your clothes again.

Keeping Control

Staying in control is very important in solving a problem. Solving a problem too quickly can cause even more problems.

Read each problem below. Then, list two ways to stay in control.

Example:

Problem: A friend agreed to go bowling with you, but then made plans to see a movie with someone else.

Ways to stay in control: _Talk to another person about the problem before doing anything._

Calmly talk the problem over with your friend.

1. Problem: You dropped your cafeteria tray. You want to run out of the cafeteria.

    Ways to stay in control: _____

    _____

2. Problem: Your mom won't let you go to a party. You want to walk out and slam the door.

    Ways to stay in control: _____

    _____

3. Problem: You're home alone at night and hear a strange noise. You want to call someone for help.

    Ways to stay in control: _____

    _____

Now, think of a problem and describe it on the lines below. Then, list two ways to stay in control.

Problem: _____

_____

Ways to stay in control: _____

_____

36

It Takes Time

When you take the time to think about your reaction to a problem, you can usually come up with a good solution.

Imagine you're angry with someone. Then, read each reaction choice below. Underline each reaction that is a quick reaction.

1. Talk to the person later in private.

2. Hit the person.

3. Tell the person you'll talk to him later when you're calmer.

4. Yell and say mean things to the person.

5. Leave the room.

6. Ask the reason in a quiet voice.

7. Explain your opinion and give reasons for it.

8. Swear at the person.

9. Throw something at the person.

10. Turn your back to the person and ignore him.

Now, think of three more ways you could show a controlled reaction to a problem. List them on the lines below. Then, share your list with someone else.

1. _____

2. _____

3. _____

37

Think!

When you solve problems, it's important to think about each solution carefully before you take action.

Read each problem below. First, decide what a quick reaction might be. Next, write a new problem that could happen because of the quick reaction. Then, write a controlled reaction to the problem.

APRIL 1990						
SUN	MON	TUE	WED	THU	FRI	SAT
	1 WORK	2	3 WORK	4	5 WORK	6
7	8 WORK	9	10 WORK	11	12 WORK	13 Go to Concert
14	15	16	17	18	19	20
21	22	23	24	25	26	27
					28	29	30

Example:

Your boss just told you that you have to work this weekend, but you've already made plans.

Quick reaction: *I'll tell my boss I'm not going to work this weekend.*

New problem: *My boss could fire me for not doing what he says.*

Controlled reaction: *Tell my boss I had made plans I can't cancel.*

1. Your teacher returned a test that you thought you'd passed. You got an *F* on the test.

   Quick reaction: _____

   New problem: _____

   Controlled reaction: _____

2. Your parents raised your brother's allowance, but not yours. You don't think that's fair.

   Quick reaction: _____

   New problem: _____

   Controlled reaction: _____

3. A salesman at the door wants to talk to your parents, who aren't home.

   Quick reaction: _____

   New problem: _____

   Controlled reaction: _____

38

ADDITIONAL ACTIVITIES

Many students need practice in looking at multiple solutions to a problem. For many, quick reactions have become habitual because they haven't examined the consequences of their actions. Use the exercises below to help your students learn the importance of using a controlled reaction to a problem.

❑ Have your students practice differentiating a quick reaction from a controlled one. Give your students a sample problem. Have them volunteer as many quick solutions as they can. Then, discuss the suggested solutions with your class and examine the possible consequences of these solutions. Follow the discussion with a look at controlled reactions to the problem. Talk about the time, energy, and money that could possibly be saved by thinking through a reaction. Also, discuss what happens to people's feelings when problems are handled too quickly.

✓ ❑ Use role-playing to help your students identify different problem solving styles. Think of several problems. Write each problem on an index card. Write the words *Quick Reaction* and *Controlled Reaction* on separate index cards, too. Have each student choose a reaction card and a problem card. Then, have him role-play the problem using the kind of reaction he chooses. Let the rest of the class try to guess the type of reaction being used. For variety, let the student also solve the problem using the opposite reaction.

❑ Discuss how quick reactions can often get a lot of attention. Have your students volunteer examples of problems that were solved with quick reactions. Then, discuss whether they got immediate attention and approval from other people. Talk about the differences between positive and negative attention.

❑ Using the same examples, talk about what might have happened if the person had thought through the problem and controlled his reaction. Discuss how some people might not even notice, while others might admire the maturity and courage it takes to think something through and resist being influenced by others. Give your students examples where it has taken courage and maturity to wait to make a decision.

Brainstorming

Good problem solving means examining all your choices before solving a problem. One way to come up with several choices is to *brainstorm* or think of as many as you can in a short amount of time.

Read each problem below. Then, have your teacher time you and see how many solutions you can think of in thirty seconds.

Example:

You found a hole in the new sweater you bought. You've never worn it.

a.   *Get a refund or exchange from the store where I bought it.*

b.   *Throw it away.*

c.   *Fix it myself.*

d.   *Wear it anyway.*

e.   *Give it away.*

1. Your parents won't buy you a telephone.

a.   _____

b.   _____

c.   _____

d.   _____

e.   _____

2. You forgot to do your math homework.

a.   _____

b.   _____

c.   _____

d.   _____

e.   _____

Now, look at your choices again for each problem. Write an **X** in front of each solution that might work. Write an **O** in front of each solution that probably won't work. Explain your decisions to someone.

Friendly Advice

Sometimes other people can help you think of solutions to problems.

Have your teacher give you a problem. Next, write at least three possible solutions on the lines below. Think of solutions that have worked for you or for someone you know.

Then, look at another student's solutions and add any different choices to your list.

1. Problem: _____

_____

Solutions:

a. _____

b. _____

c. _____

d. _____

e. _____

Solutions from another student:

f. _____

g. _____

h. _____

Did it help to look at someone else's ideas? _____ Explain your answer.

_____

Did you get any new ideas from sharing? _____ What were they?

_____

_____

On Your Mark

You can often think of several good solutions to a problem if you work together with someone else.

Choose someone to work with. Next, have your teacher give you a problem to solve. Then, with the other student, list at least five solutions. Have your teacher time you if you'd like.

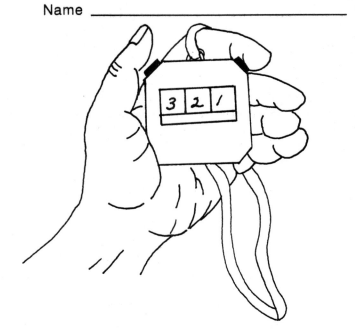

Problem: _____

_____

Solutions:

    1. _____

    2. _____

    3. _____

    4. _____

    5. _____

Time: _____

List some more solutions.

    6. _____

    7. _____

    8. _____

Now, read your list of solutions again. Draw a circle around the three best solutions.

Does it help to work with someone else? _____ Explain your answer.

_____

Many students need considerable practice in looking at alternative solutions to problems. They sometimes aren't aware of the flexibility and creativity needed to solve problems. To help your students stretch their thinking and planning skills, use the exercises below. With additional practice, your students will learn to look at multiple solutions to a problem and to enlist a variety of available resources to make their problem solving efforts more effective.

❏ Provide your students with a sample problem. Then, see how many solutions they can think of in a given amount of time. Encourage your students to think of realistic solutions. When time is up, have them record their solutions on a piece of paper. In a class discussion, ask which student has the most solutions and then have him share the solutions with the rest of the class. Let your students vote on the best solution, discussing the pros and cons of each one.

❏ Play a game of *Dueling Choices*. Divide your students into pairs. Next, ask each pair to set a goal of solution choices they'd like to meet for a problem you'll give them. Then, read a problem and give them two minutes to reach their goal. The team choosing the highest goal can earn five points. If they don't reach their goal, the team with the next highest goal has an opportunity to earn the points. Award additional points for solution choices the other team didn't have.

❏ To give your students more practice in differentiating between realistic solution choices and impossible choices, give them several problems to solve. Each time you give them a problem, have them generate two realistic choices and one impossible choice. Follow with a discussion of what makes a solution choice realistic and what makes a solution an unwise choice.

43

What Helps?

Solving a problem is easier when you know your resources. Remember that a resource can be money, an object, or someone who can help you.

Read each item listed. Then, write an **X** before each resource you have, and an **O** before each resource you don't have.

_____ 1. old shoes

_____ 2. paper

_____ 3. telephone

_____ 4. a car

_____ 5. a brother or sister

_____ 6. a nail

_____ 7. a knife

_____ 8. an extra bed

_____ 9. a bike

_____ 10. $100

_____ 11. carpenter tools

_____ 12. a computer

_____ 13. a favorite teacher

_____ 14. a TV

_____ 15. one of your parents

_____ 16. a dog

_____ 17. a box

_____ 18. a C.B. radio

_____ 19. a belt

_____ 20. a watch

_____ 21. $10

_____ 22. a friend

_____ 23. soap

_____ 24. some free time

_____ 25. extra food

Resources Inside You

Name _____

Some resources for solving problems are inside you, like special talents or personality traits.

Read the list of resources below. Then, put an **X** in front of the talents or personality traits that describe you. Underline the ones you wish you had.

1. _____ I'm patient.

2. _____ I have lots of energy.

3. _____ I can talk to people easily.

4. _____ I can ask people questions.

5. _____ I'm good at sports.

6. _____ I'm a hard worker.

7. _____ I'm honest.

8. _____ I'm creative.

9. _____ I can work on something until it's done.

10. _____ I like to read the newspaper and magazines.

11. _____ I learn quickly.

12. _____ I'm a good listener.

13. _____ I like to figure things out.

14. _____ I'm good at fixing things.

15. _____ I take time to think things through.

16. _____ I care how other people feel.

17. _____ I like to write letters.

18. _____ I'm good at remembering people's names.

19. _____ I'm comfortable talking with people of all ages.

20. _____ I like to use the phone.

Now, draw a circle around the numbers of the resources you think are the most important to have. Discuss the reasons for your choices with the rest of the class.

Past Successes

It's easier to solve a problem if you've solved one like it before.

Read each problem below. Decide if you've ever had a problem like that. If you have, explain what you did to solve it. Ask a parent or a friend if you don't remember. Later, share your past successes with someone else.

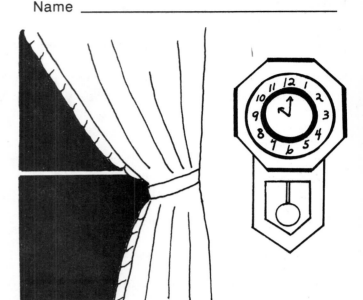

1. You came home later than you told your parents. Your parents are mad.

   Has this ever happened to you?   Yes   No

   How did you solve it? _____

   _____

   Did the solution work? Explain your answer. _____

   _____

2. You lost something that belonged to someone else.

   Has this ever happened to you?   Yes   No

   How did you solve it? _____

   _____

   Did the solution work? Explain your answer. _____

   _____

3. You didn't finish your homework on time.

   Has this ever happened to you?   Yes   No

   How did you solve it? _____

   _____

   Did the solution work? Explain your answer. _____

   _____

46

Experience Counts

Name _____

When you solve a problem, it helps to talk to someone who's had a similar problem.

Read each problem below. Next, decide which person you could talk to who has had a similar experience. Then, write the letter of your choice on the blank. You can use an answer more than once. Remember that your opinions may be different from someone else's opinions.

_____ 1. You run out of milk when you're making pudding for dessert.

_____ 2. You're not sure how to ask someone for a date.

_____ 3. You permed your own hair and it doesn't look good.

_____ 4. You aren't getting along with your boss.

_____ 5. You don't know how to handle a child you're babysitting.

_____ 6. You don't know how to fix your bike.

_____ 7. Two of your friends aren't getting along. One of them wants you to take her side.

_____ 8. You're taking a math class that's very hard. You have a test soon.

_____ 9. Your brother picks on you when your parents aren't home.

_____ 10. A group of older students picks on you in the cafeteria.

a. your older sister

b. your father

c. your mother

d. a fellow worker

e. your older brother

f. a friend

g. another student

h. a neighbor

Who else do you know that could help you solve a problem?

47

Creative Solutions

Sometimes you may want someone to help you solve a problem. Read each problem below. Think of solutions that involve someone else's help. Then, answer each question below.

1. You got your hair cut and it looks awful.

    Who could you talk to? _____

    What would you say to this person? _____

    _____

    What could you ask a friend to do? _____

    _____

    What could you do next time? _____

    _____

2. You were caught talking to a friend during a test. The teacher took the test away and gave you an *F*.

    Who could you talk to? _____

    What would you say to this person? _____

    _____

    What could you ask a friend to do? _____

    _____

    What could you do next time? _____

    _____

Describe a problem you had when you asked for someone else's help. Share your example with someone.

48

What Do I Need?

If you know your resources, it's easier to choose a solution to a problem.

Read each problem below. Then, list three resources you need to solve the problem. Remember that a resource can be money, an object, a person, a talent, a personality trait, or a past experience.

Example:

You need to cut down a tree.

Resources: a.   *a chain saw*

               b.   *someone who knows how to cut down a tree*

               c.   *money to pay the person*

1. You need to clean your room.

Resources: a.   _____

               b.   _____

               c.   _____

2. You need to pack for a vacation.

Resources: a.   _____

               b.   _____

               c.   _____

3. You need to buy a present for your mother's birthday.

Resources: a.   _____

               b.   _____

               c.   _____

4. You and a friend just had an argument. You want to make up.

Resources: a.   _____

               b.   _____

               c.   _____

ADDITIONAL ACTIVITIES

Your students need to be able to evaluate the solutions they generate. They must decide if a solution is realistic and if they have the resources to carry it out. Students must also be willing to ask questions to obtain necessary information and to look at their own and others' past successes with problem solving. Give your students practice with these important skills by using the activities below.

❏ Divide your students into pairs. Next, give each pair a problem to solve and have each student write three possible solutions. Tell the partners to exchange solutions and decide if each solution is realistic. As your students evaluate solutions, encourage them to ask their partners questions to obtain any information they need to evaluate the solution. Have them delete solutions that aren't realistic and be ready to explain why they aren't realistic in a follow-up class discussion.

❏ Arrange your students in a circle. Give them a problem that requires material resources. Next, go around the circle and ask each student to name a material needed to solve the problem. Students who give a resource can earn a point. Give points around the circle until ideas are exhausted. Keep score on a piece of paper or on a chalkboard or overhead projector.

❏ To encourage your students to ask others for help, have them think of people they could go to for help. Tell each of them to list three people they'd go to for help. Have them write each person's name and a reason this person might be helpful. Then, give your students a sample problem. Have them choose one of the three people to ask for help and explain why. Let them choose someone other than those they originally listed if other people come to mind.

❏ Give your students practice in examining past successes and experiences as resources for solving future problems. Have each student bring in three examples of problems they've seen on TV. Encourage them to bring examples of problems faced by TV characters to make the discussion easier. Then, discuss the examples and ask your students to relate their own past experiences to the problems. Examine solutions they used for similar problems. Ask them to look at the solution that worked and decide if it will work in this situation.

Do the same activity, but use examples of childhood dilemmas. Ask your students to think about their own experiences or those of someone else. Have them look at the best possible solution for each dilemma, based on their experiences.

Throw It Out!

If you have many possible solutions to a problem, you want to choose the best one. Don't use solutions that ask for resources you don't have.

Read each problem below. Compare the list of resources you need with the resources you have. Circle the resources you don't have. Then, circle the letter of the solution that won't work.

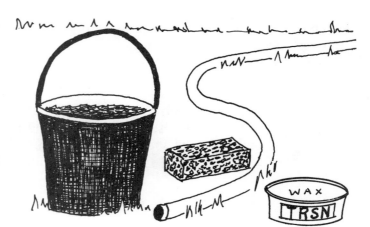

Example:

Problem: You have to wash the mud off your dad's car.

Resources you need: soap, bucket, (brush,) water, (hose,) good weather, towels

Resources you have: soap, bucket, water, good weather, towels

Solutions: a. Put soap and water in the bucket, wash the car and then rinse it with more water.

(b.) Fill the bucket, wash the car, rinse it with a hose, dry it, and wax it.

c. Wash the car, rinse it by filling the bucket again, and then dry it.

Problem: You have a bad sunburn.

Resources you need: lotion, aspirin, a cool shower, a bed, a cool drink

Resources you have: a cool shower, a bed, a cool drink

Solutions: a. Put on lotion and relax.

b. Take a cool shower and lie on the bed.

c. Have a cool drink and go to bed early.

Now, make up a problem. List the resources you need and the resources you have. Next, think of three solutions to the problem. Then, choose the best solution by comparing the resources you need with the resources you have.

Problem: _____

Resources you need: _____

Resources you have: _____

Solutions: a. _____

b. _____

c. _____

Time, Energy, and Money

Name _____

Solving a problem can take time, energy, and money. Read each problem below. Then, guess how much time, energy, or money it will take to use each solution suggested.

Keep in mind that your opinions may be different from someone else's opinions. Later, share your opinions with the rest of the class.

Example:

You have to mow your lawn.

A.   Solution: You'll cut the lawn with a push mower.

Time _2 hours_   Energy _lots_   Money _none_

B.   Solution: You'll use a power mower to cut the lawn.

Time _1/2 hour_   Energy _some_   Money _none_

1.   You want to buy your brother a cassette tape player for his birthday.

A.   Solution: You'll compare prices at several stores and then buy him a cassette tape player.

Time _____   Energy _____   Money _____

B.   Solution: You'll buy a cassette player you saw on sale in the paper.

Time _____   Energy _____   Money _____

2.   Your friend can't give you a ride to school this morning.

A.   Solution: You'll walk the half mile to school.

Time _____   Energy _____   Money _____

B.   Solution: You'll take the city bus to school.

Time _____   Energy _____   Money _____

Is This for Real?

After you examine all the solutions to a problem, you need to choose solutions that are likely to work.

Read each problem below. Rate each solution by writing **Yes** before a solution that will probably work. Write **No** before a solution that isn't likely to work.

As you read each solution, think about what you need to carry it out, like tools or materials, help from someone, or extra money.

1. You were absent from school and missed some important notes in a class. You need to know them for a test coming up.

    Solutions: _____ a.   Borrow a friend's notes.

                    _____ b.   Have a friend recopy her notes for you.

                    _____ c.   Ask your teacher to give you the notes.

                    _____ d.   On the day of the test, tell your teacher you didn't get the notes.

2. You have no new clothes for school.

    Solutions: _____ a.   Sew some new clothes.

                    _____ b.   Borrow some clothes from a friend.

                    _____ c.   Get a job and buy your clothes.

                    _____ d.   Ask your mom for $150 to buy some clothes.

3. You don't have a ride to a party that is 5 miles away.

    Solutions: _____ a.   Walk to the party.

                    _____ b.   Call a friend who's going and ask him for a ride.

                    _____ c.   Take your parents' car.

                    _____ d.   Ask your brother or sister to drive you.

Can you think of other choices that might work for each problem above? Write two more solutions for each problem on the back of this page. Decide which solution is best and why.

Will It Work?

When you solve a problem, you need to examine every possible solution to make the right choice.

Read each problem below. Then, circle the letter of each solution that would be a good way to solve the problem.

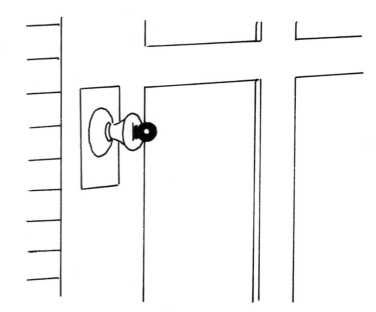

1. You lost your house key.

    a. Blame your sister for stealing it.

    b. Look everywhere you've been that day.

    c. Don't tell anyone.

    d. Ask your family if anyone has seen it.

    e. Borrow your parents' key and get a new copy made.

2. Your bike has a flat tire.

    a. Blame your brother for leaving nails out in the garage.

    b. Ask your mom for money to have the tire fixed.

    c. Call a friend and complain about your bike.

    d. Ask your sister if you can borrow her bike until yours is fixed.

    e. Put the bike away in the garage.

3. You're babysitting your little sister and gum gets stuck in her hair.

    a. Cut her hair where the gum is stuck.

    b. Leave the gum in her hair until your parents get home and then tell them.

    c. Try to comb the gum out.

    d. Leave the gum in her hair and hope she tells someone else about it.

    e. Call someone that might be able to tell you how to get it out.

How do you decide which ways would be good to solve a problem? _____

_____

It's Impossible!

When you compare solutions, you have to look for solutions that will work.

Read each problem below. Put **No** in the blank if it's a solution that won't work and explain your reason. Remember that your opinions may be different from someone else's opinions.

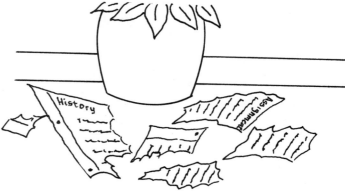

Example:

   Problem: You tore up your homework by mistake. Now, you need to hand it in.

   _No_   Solution: Tape the pieces back together and hand it in.

   Why won't this solution work?   *The teacher will only take neat papers.*

1. Problem: You broke a neighbor's window.

   _____   Solution: Nail boards over the window.

   Why won't this solution work? _____

   _____

2. Problem: You missed two weeks of school.

   _____   Solution: Go back to school and forget about the work you missed.

   Why won't this solution work? _____

   _____

3. Problem: The car is dirty.

   _____   Solution: Take the car to a car wash.

   Why won't this solution work? _____

   _____

4. Problem: You lost your friend's cassette tape player.

   _____   Solution: Tell your friend that someone took it.

   Why won't this solution work? _____

   _____

Looking Ahead

When you compare solutions to a problem, you need to think about what might happen if you choose a certain solution. Sometimes a solution can cause a new problem.

Read each problem and solution below. Then, answer each question.

1. Someone keeps calling you and you've asked him to stop. You decide to change your phone number.

   Would this solution cause a new problem?   Yes   No   Explain your answer.

   _____

2. You don't like your new hairstyle. You decide to get your hair cut for the third time this month.

   Would this solution cause a new problem?   Yes   No   Explain your answer.

   _____

3. Your sister lies to your mom about things you do. You decide to tell your mom she's lying.

   Would this solution cause a new problem?   Yes   No   Explain your answer.

   _____

4. You need to have a research paper typed for class. You've found someone to do it for $1 a page.

   Would this solution cause a new problem?   Yes   No   Explain your answer.

   _____

5. Your parents aren't home to fix dinner and you're hungry. You decide to cook something for yourself.

   Would this solution cause a new problem?   Yes   No   Explain your answer.

   _____

The Good and the Bad

Name _____

When you choose a solution, you need to consider every part of it.

Read the problem below. Next, look at all the things to consider about the possible solution. Put a **G** in the blank if it's good, and a **B** if it's not. Then, decide if the solution is a good one for the problem.

Problem: Your parents can't give you rides to school and work.

Solution: Look into buying a used car you can drive yourself.

Things to consider:

_____ The car costs $150.

_____ The car has a radio.

_____ The car has the tires it had when it was new.

_____ The heater doesn't work.

_____ The car has a lot of room.

_____ Your parents will let you buy it.

_____ The car doesn't have air conditioning.

_____ The car has some rust on the fenders.

_____ The car has new spark plugs.

_____ The muffler was just replaced.

_____ You like the color of the car.

_____ The car uses a lot of gas.

Is this a good solution to the problem? Explain your answer.

Evaluating Solutions   57

Pros and Cons

Name _____

When you look at possible solutions to a problem, you need to consider the pros and cons of each one. A *pro* is a reason the solution will work. A *con* is a reason the solution might not work.

Read each problem below. Then, look at the information about the solution. If the information is a pro, put a **P** in the blank. If it's a con, put a **C** in the blank.

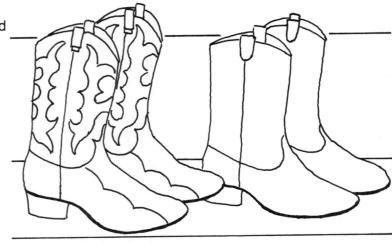

Example:

You can't choose between two pairs of boots.

_____P_____ Information: One pair of boots has more style than the other.

1. You can't decide if you should perm your hair.

   _____ Information: The perm would cost $80.

2. A friend wants you to try smoking cigarettes.

   _____ Information: You could get cancer if you make it a habit.

3. You have homework to do, but your favorite show is on TV.

   _____ Information: You earn a grade for homework.

4. A friend needs help fixing his car, but you'd rather go bowling.

   _____ Information: Your friend may like you more.

5. You've been offered a part-time job.

   _____ Information: You need a ride to get there.

6. You've been invited to a surprise party on the same night you were invited to a movie.

   _____ Information: The surprise party is for a good friend.

7. You have math and history assignments to do.

   _____ Information: The math assignment isn't due for two days.

8. Your next door neighbor needs someone to babysit.

   _____ Information: You need the money.

Pick the Best

When you compare solutions to a problem, you have to look at the pros and cons of each one.

Read the problem and solutions below. Then, add your own ideas to the list of pros and cons for each solution. Next, compare the solutions and choose the one you think would be better.

Example: | Problem: You need dressy clothes for a school dance. |

Solution A: Make them yourself.

PROS:

1.   *I like to sew.*

2.   *No one else will have the same clothes.*

3.   *I can save money.*

CONS:

1.   *It will take time to sew.*

2.   *I might not find a pattern I like.*

3.   *I might not find fabric I like.*

Solution B: Buy some new clothes.

PROS:

1.   *I can get them right away.*

2.   *I like to shop.*

3.   *I can get a popular style.*

CONS:

1.   *Someone else may have the same clothes.*

2.   *They'll cost a lot of money.*

3.   *I need a ride to the store.*

Which solution is a better choice?   Solution A   (Solution B)

| Problem: You have an English assignment due tomorrow. |

Solution A: Do the assignment at home.

PROS:

1.   *Your parents can help you.*

2.   _____

3.   _____

CONS:

1.   *It takes up your free time.*

2.   _____

3.   _____

Solution B: Do the assignment during lunch.

PROS:

1.   *You can get it done at school.*

2.   _____

3.   _____

CONS:

1.   *You can't be with your friends.*

2.   _____

3.   _____

Which solution is a better choice?   Solution A   Solution B

It Takes Practice

As you practice solving problems, choosing the best solution gets easier. Try to solve the problem below.

First, write possible solutions for the problem. Give the pros and cons of each one.

Next, list the resources the person has and the resources he needs. Then, decide which solution is a better choice.

Problem: Jim tried out for the basketball team, but he didn't make it. He wants to play sports, but he's afraid to try out for another team. Jim is 5 feet tall. He's quick and he's a good team player.

Solution A: _____

PROS:

1. _____

2. _____

3. _____

CONS:

1. _____

2. _____

3. _____

Resources he has:

1. _____

2. _____

3. _____

Solution B: _____

PROS:

1. _____

2. _____

3. _____

CONS:

1. _____

2. _____

3. _____

Resources he needs:

1. _____

2. _____

3. _____

Which solution is a better choice? Why? _____

_____

Evaluating Solutions   60

It's Your Turn

When you look at solutions, you need to compare the pros and cons of each one. Then, you can choose the better solution.

Think of a problem you have right now. Write the problem in the box below. Next, write two possible solutions to the problem.

Then, list the pros and cons of each solution. List the resources you have and the resources you need, too. Finally, choose the better solution for the problem by comparing your choices.

Problem: _____

_____

Solution A: _____   **Solution B:** _____

PROS: PROS:

1. _____   1. _____

2. _____   2. _____

3. _____   3. _____

CONS: CONS:

1. _____   1. _____

2. _____   2. _____

3. _____   3. _____

Resources you have: Resources you need:

1. _____   2. _____

2. _____   2. _____

3. _____   3. _____

Which solution is a better choice?   Why? _____

_____

ADDITIONAL ACTIVITIES

Choosing the better solution to a problem is a difficult step in problem solving. It requires students to generate and weigh the pros and cons of each solution, consider their resources, and then decide which solution is most workable. To help your students gain confidence and expertise in evaluating solutions, use the activities below.

❑ Divide your students into small groups. Give each group a concrete problem and ask them to generate several solutions to the problem. Have them write their solutions on a chalkboard. Next, ask them to narrow their choices of solutions to two by listing the pros and cons of each solution on the chalkboard. Then, have the group compare the pros and cons and vote on the better solution.

❑ Have each student think of a problem and write it on an index card. Next, collect the cards and give one to each student. On the back of the card, have each student write two possible solutions and a list of three pros and three cons for each solution. Remind them to think of the time, energy, and money involved in each solution. Then, have each student choose the better solution. When everyone is finished, have your students share their problems and solutions in a class discussion.

❑ Teach your students to predict new problems that might be caused by a given solution. Choose two students to listen to a problem. Have one student give a solution that won't create a new problem, while the other student gives a solution that will create a new problem.

   Students listening to the solutions should then figure out which solution is better. Have them also offer possible new problems caused by the negative solution.

❑ Divide your students into pairs. Give each pair a set of five problems to solve. Ask them to think of the better solution for each problem, along with a *backup* or alternative solution. Encourage them to weigh the pros and the cons, and discuss any new problems that might arise. Follow the activity with a class discussion about the problems and the reasons for their choices.

PLANS

Goal:　To plan how to initiate a solution.

OBJECTIVES

PLANNING THE STEPS:　　　　To understand the importance of planning and organizing a solution.

ENLISTING RESOURCES:　　　To assess and enlist the resources for carrying out a solution.

SEEING OTHERS' VIEWPOINTS:　To consider others' viewpoints and needs when enlisting help.

TAKING THE FIRST STEP:　　　To take the first step in a solution.

This section of *Problem Solving for Teens* contains exercises for your students in choosing and organizing a solution plan and then identifying the first step for putting the plan into action. These exercises will help your students recognize the need for planning to ensure successful problem solving.

TEACHING SUGGESTIONS

1. Discuss why people need to plan before acting on problems. Have a class discussion about the uses of planning in everyday life. Discuss activities like planning meals, vacations, classroom lessons, parties, having a budget, and constructing things.

2. To illustrate the consequences of poor planning, let your students share examples of problems resulting from a lack of planning. Discuss the costs involved in poor planning, like damaged possessions, hurt feelings, wasted time and wasted money.

3. Before doing the exercises in this unit, review sequencing skills with your students. Discuss concepts like *before, during, after, first, second, third, beginning, middle* and *end* so your students understand the step-by-step nature of planning a solution.

4. Teach your students the importance of asking questions when they plan a solution. Remind them of the *WH* questions they need to ask to thoroughly plan every step of a solution. They can ask questions like:

    Who can help me with my plan?
    What resources do I need?
    When is the best time to carry out each step?
    Where do I need to go?
    Why do I need to do it a certain way?
    How can I make the plan go smoothly?

5. Have your students practice thinking flexibly when they look at the resources they have and the resources they need for solving a problem. Give your students concrete examples in which material items have been used in ways other than they were designed for, like using a pair of scissors to poke a hole or using a rock to pound something in. Bring in office and household items as examples to talk about.

6. Encourage your students to write down the steps of a solution to ensure that every step is planned and remembered. With practice, they'll be able to mentally plan solutions.

7. When you discuss others' points of view, let your students volunteer their own examples of family members that they've asked for help. Talk about the importance of considering another's point of view, his mood, and the best time or place to approach him when enlisting help. Discuss the need to be sensitive to one another's needs.

8. Discuss the meaning of *action* in problem solving. Action means planning the solution to a problem and then taking the first step. Remind your students that although taking the first step is difficult, planning and organizing will make things go smoothly.

Make a List

Listing the smaller steps to a solution plan can help you remember everything you need to do to solve a problem.

Read the problem and solution below.   Then, list the steps you'd follow to solve the problem. Two steps are listed for you.

Problem: Your room is very messy.

Solution: Clean it now before it gets messier.

Steps:

1.   *Pick up dirty dishes and take them to the kitchen.* _____

2.   *Make my bed.* _____

3.   _____

4.   _____

5.   _____

6.   _____

7.   _____

8.   _____

9.   _____

10.   _____

What would you do first if you had to clean your room?   Explain why.

_____

_____

Planning Resources

Listing the steps in a solution plan can help you decide what resources you need, too.

Read the problem and solution below. Next, list the steps you'll follow to solve the problem. Then, write the resources you'll need to do each step.   Remember that resources can be materials, money, or people you need to help solve the problem.   One step and resource are listed for you.

Problem: You have a research report due for science class in two days, but you don't know what to write about.

Solution: Choose a topic for the report and do the research today.

Steps:

1. _____
2. _____
3. _____
4. _____
5. _____
6. _____
7. _____
8. _____
9. _____
10.   *Write the research report.* _____

Resources needed:

1.   *library books, encyclopedias* _____
2. _____
3. _____
4. _____
5. _____

66

Ordering the Steps

As you list the steps of a solution plan, you need to decide the order in which to do them. Decide what to do *before* other activities, *during* the main activity, and then *after* the main activity.

Read the problem below.   Next, read the solution.   Then, list the steps below when you need to do them.   Some of the steps are done for you.

> Problem: Your best friend is moving away and you want her to know you'll miss her.

Solution: Take your friend to a restaurant for a going-away dinner.

Steps:

Before the dinner:

_____ a. *Call a restaurant to reserve a table for the party.* _____

_____ b. _____

_____ c. _____

During the dinner:

_____ d. *Make sure my friend is served well.* _____

_____ e. _____

_____ f. _____

After the dinner:

_____ g. *Give my friend a going-away present.* _____

_____ h. _____

_____ i. _____

Now, decide the order to do these steps.   Write a **1** on the blank in front of the first step, a **2** by the second step, and so on.

67

Organizing the Steps

To follow a solution plan, you need to know when to do each step. Think about what to do *before* other activities, *during* the main activity, and *after* the main activity.

Read the problem below.   Next, read the solution.   Then, list the steps below when you need to do them.

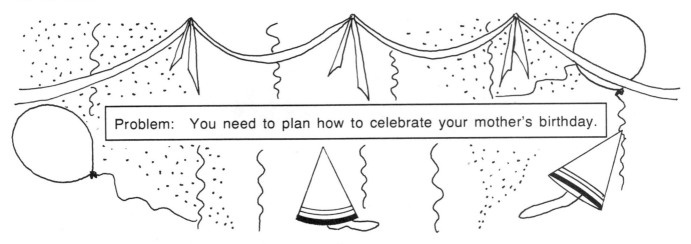

Problem: You need to plan how to celebrate your mother's birthday.

Solution: Give a party for my mother at our house.

Steps:

Before the party:

_____   a. _____

_____   b. _____

_____   c. _____

During the party:

_____   d. _____

_____   e. _____

_____   f. _____

After the party:

_____   g. _____

_____   h. _____

_____   i. _____

What order should you follow in your plan?   Write a **1** on the blank in front of the first step, a **2** by what you'd do second, and so on.

How Long?

When you make a solution plan, you need to know how much time each step will take.

Read each step below. Next, decide how long each step would take you if it were part of your solution plan. Then, write the time in the blank after the step. Remember that your times may be different from someone else's times.

Time

1. Go to the hardware store. _____

2. Take the garbage out. _____

3. Walk to a friend's house. _____

4. Borrow money from someone in your family. _____

5. Clean your room. _____

6. Call a friend for advice. _____

7. Get ready for a party. _____

8. Do your homework on a school night. _____

9. Look for a lost item in your room. _____

10. Call a friend to apologize. _____

11. Shop for a present for someone. _____

12. Cook supper for a brother or sister and you. _____

13. Call a restaurant to make a reservation. _____

14. Research a topic at the library. _____

15. Help your dad clean the garage. _____

Now, share your answers with a classmate. Compare the amount of time you've written for each step. Discuss the reasons for your choices.

What's First?

Some steps are best to do at the beginning.
In other cases, it may be best to do a step at
a certain time because it leads to another step.

Read each problem below. Next, decide the
order in which to do each step. Then, write **1**
in front of the first step, and so on.

1. Problem: You have no one to cook your dinner.

    Solution: Make my own peanut butter and jelly sandwich.

    Steps: _____ Get out a glass and pour milk in it.

    _____ Get out the bread.

    _____ Cut the sandwich in half.

    _____ Spread the peanut butter.

    _____ Put the two slices of bread together.

    _____ Put jelly on the bread.

2. Problem: There aren't any clean dishes for dinner.

    Solution: Clean the dirty dishes.

    Steps: _____ Fill the sink with hot, soapy water.

    _____ Dry the clean dishes.

    _____ Put away the clean dishes or put them on the table for dinner.

    _____ Wash and rinse the dirty dishes.

    _____ Put the dirty dishes in the sink.

3. Problem: A button popped off your shirt.

    Solution: Sew the button on my shirt.

    Steps: _____ Knot and cut the thread.

    _____ Sew through the button holes and the shirt.

    _____ Thread a needle and tie a knot in the thread.

    _____ Position the button on the shirt.

Question, Please!

Asking questions can help you decide what to do in a solution plan. By asking questions like *who, what, where, when, why*, and *how*, you'll be able to solve a problem successfully.

Read the problem below. Then, answer each question. Give more than one answer if you need to. Later, share your answers in a class discussion.

REPORT CARD

	1ST Quarter	2ND Quarter	3RD Quarter	4TH Quarter
ENGLISH	B			
MATH	F			
HISTORY	C			
SCIENCE	B			
P.E.	B			
MUSIC	B			

DAYS ABSENT	0			
TIMES TARDY	1			
HONOR POINTS				

Problem: You're failing a class.

Solution: Get extra help.

WHO can give me extra help? _____

_____

WHAT should I do to get the extra help? _____

_____

WHERE can I get extra help? _____

_____

WHEN would be the best time to ask for help? _____

_____

WHEN would be the best time to get the extra help? _____

_____

WHY should my teacher be involved? _____

_____

HOW can I make sure the extra help is working? _____

_____

WHAT should be my first step to solve this problem? _____

_____

71

Step by Step

Name _____

When you plan a solution to a problem, you decide the steps to follow and the order in which to do them.

Read each problem and solution below. Next, decide what steps you'll follow and the order in which you'll do them. Remember to ask yourself questions as you plan. The first step is done for you.

Problem: You don't know anyone in your English class.

Solution: Start a conversation with someone in class.

Steps:

1.   *Choose one person from the class that I'd like to know.* _____

2.   _____

3.   _____

4.   _____

Is every step in the right order?   Yes   No   If not, renumber the steps in the right order.

What question could you ask to check your planning?

_____

Will the problem be solved after you follow all the steps?   Yes   No

Problem: Your little sister keeps getting into your things.

Solution: Put my things away where she can't get them.

Steps:

1.   *Decide what things need to be put out of her reach.* _____

2.   _____

3.   _____

4.   _____

Is every step in the right order?   Yes   No   If not, renumber the steps in the right order.

What question could you ask to check your planning?

_____

Will the problem be solved after you follow all the steps?   Yes   No

72

ADDITIONAL ACTIVITIES

Planning the steps of a solution involves sequencing the steps and asking questions. Students need practice thinking through their ideas. The activities below will help your students better organize their solution plans.

❏ Ask your students to list three ways organizing is used in situations at home and school. Some possible examples are: appointments written on a calendar, lists of each family member's chores, and daily homework assignment books. Encourage students to discuss why organizing is important in these instances.

❏ Challenge your students to ask questions as they plan. Give a problem and solution to the class. Let your students have one minute to list the steps in their solution plans. Next, each student asks another student a question to see if the answer has been included in the plan. If the information is missing, the student asking the questions gets a point. If the information is present, the student who answered the question gets a point. Continue until all students have been asked a question once. Then, present a new problem and solution and repeat the process. The first student who earns five points is the winner.

Vary the challenge by asking your students the *WH* question yourself. Ask more concrete questions for those students experiencing difficulty. If a student has not provided the information, use the opportunity to provide corrective feedback. If you wish to keep score, have yourself be one team and the students be a second team. Give yourself one point if a student has not provided the information. Give the students a point if the information is present. The team with the most points wins.

❏ To provide practice sequencing the steps of a solution plan, play a game with two teams. A pair of students from each team goes up to the chalkboard. You state a problem and solution. One member of the pair writes a quick plan of action in four steps. Then, the other member numbers the steps in the best sequential order. After both members have returned to their seats, assign each team up to three points for completeness, ordering, and quickness. The team with the most points wins.

Be Prepared

Some problems need to be solved by using tools or other materials.

Read each problem and solution below. List the materials or tools you need. Next, circle whether you have each item, or whether you need to get it.

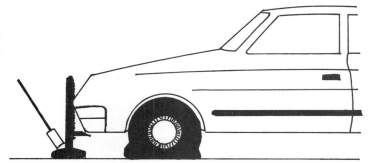

Problem: On the way home from work, your car has a flat tire.

Solution: Change the flat tire.

Materials:

1. _____   Have it.   Need to get it.

2. _____   Have it.   Need to get it.

3. _____   Have it.   Need to get it.

4. _____   Have it.   Need to get it.

5. _____   Have it.   Need to get it.

Problem: You need to write a paper for science class.

Solution: Write the paper on cholesterol.

Materials:

1. _____   Have it.   Need to get it.

2. _____   Have it.   Need to get it.

3. _____   Have it.   Need to get it.

4. _____   Have it.   Need to get it.

5. _____   Have it.   Need to get it.

You Need Time

Besides listing the materials you'll need, you need to know how long each step of a solution will take. Then, you can plan how much time you need to solve the problem.

Read the problem and solution below. Next, write how long you need to complete each step. Then, list the materials needed. The first step is done for you.

Problem: Dad won't be home to cook dinner.

Solution: Cook dinner myself.

Steps: Materials:

1. Make the salad.   _bowl, lettuce, tomatoes, cucumber, radishes,_

   Time   _15 minutes_   _green pepper, knife_

2. Make the spaghetti sauce.   _____

   Time _____   _____

3. Cook the noodles.   _____

   Time _____   _____

4. Set the table.   _____

   Time _____   _____

5. Put the food on the table.   _____

   Time _____   _____

Who Can Help?

Other people can help you as you plan a solution.

Read each problem, solution, and set of steps below. Next, list each person you would need to talk to and how you would contact that person. The first problem is done for you.

Problem: You broke a lamp at home.

Solution: Buy a new lamp.

Steps: 1. Tell your parents you broke the lamp and will replace it.

2. Ask your boss if you can work extra hours.

3. Ask your parents where they bought the lamp.

4. Find out if that store has another lamp in stock.

5. After you get paid, buy the lamp.

Person you need to talk to	How to contact that person
parents	*Talk to them at home.*
boss	*Call her up or talk to her at work.*
store clerk	*Call him at the furniture store.*

Problem: You don't have a ride to the football game.

Solution: Ask your mother or a friend to give you a ride.

Steps: 1. Ask your mother for a ride.

2. If your mother says no, then ask a friend for a ride.

3. Arrange a time to get the ride from your friend.

4. Ask your mother for permission to ride with your friend.

Person you need to talk to	How to contact that person
_____	_____
_____	_____
_____	_____

Chart Your Path

Name _____

Sometimes you need to map out where you're going when you solve a problem, so you don't retrace your steps or make extra trips.

Read the problem and solution below. Next, use the map of the school building to decide the order in which each step should be done. Write a **1** in front of the first step, and so on.

Problem: You're in study hall, and the secretary in the school office asks you to get each room's attendance slip right away.

Solution: Collect the slips and give them to the secretary.

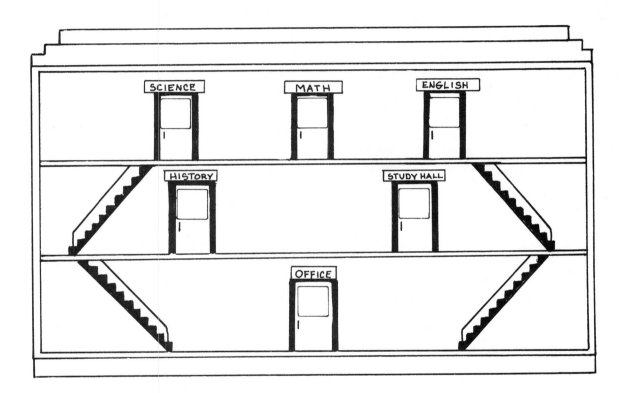

Steps:

_____ Collect the math room attendance slip.

_____ Collect the study hall attendance slip.

_____ Take the slips to the school office.

_____ Collect the science room attendance slip.

_____ Collect the history room attendance slip.

_____ Collect the English room attendance slip.

Make a Map

When you need to visit several places to solve a problem, it's important to plan where you're going to help you save time and energy.

Read the problem and solution below. Next, use the map to decide the order in which each step should be done. Write a **1** in front of the first step, and so on.

Problem: You're going to Florida on vacation and you need to get some supplies.

Solution: On my way home from work, I'll stop to get these supplies.

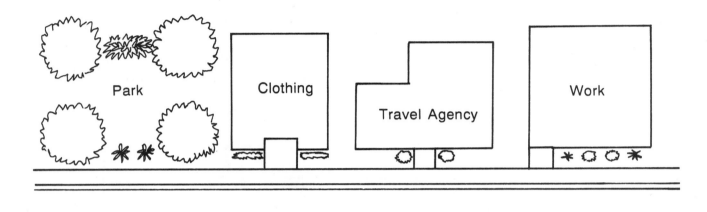

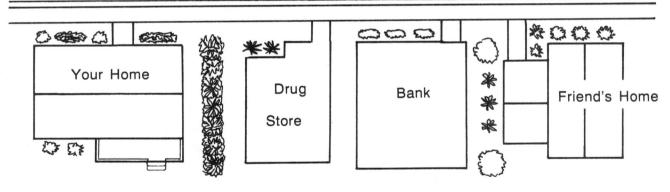

Steps:

_____   Buy suntan lotion at the drugstore.

_____   Get money out of my bank account.

_____   Borrow a suitcase from my sister.

_____   Buy a new swimsuit and a pair of shorts.

_____   Get my plane tickets at the travel agent.

_____   Borrow a Walkman from my friend.

78

Put It All Together

Name _____

Now it's time to practice all the steps of making a solution plan.

Read the problem and solution below. Next, list the steps you would take, the materials you need, and the time you need for each step. Then, write a **1** in front of the first step, and so on.

Problem: Your bike has a bent rear reflector and a flat tire.

Solution: Fix the bike myself.

Steps:

_____ 1. _____

            Materials: _____

            Time: _____

_____ 2. _____

            Materials: _____

            Time: _____

_____ 3. _____

            Materials: _____

            Time: _____

_____ 4. _____

            Materials: _____

            Time: _____

_____ 5. _____

            Materials: _____

            Time: _____

Solving a Real Problem

Name _____

Everyone has problems to solve. Think about a problem you have now with your friends, your family, at school, or at work. List the problem below. Next, choose a solution. Then, list the steps you can take to solve the problem, and the materials and time needed for each step. Then, write a **1** in front of the first step, and so on.

Problem: _____

Solution: _____

Steps:

_____   1. _____

   Materials: _____

   Time: _____

_____   2. _____

   Materials: _____

   Time: _____

_____   3. _____

   Materials: _____

   Time: _____

_____   4. _____

   Materials: _____

   Time: _____

_____   5. _____

   Materials: _____

   Time: _____

Now, follow your plan to solve the problem. Did the plan work to solve your problem? Why or why not?

_____

_____

What step in your plan would you change, if any? Explain why.

_____

_____

ADDITIONAL ACTIVITIES

Organizing a solution plan and enlisting the needed resources is crucial to successfully solving problems. As your students plan the steps, they need to consider the important materials and time needed. Your students also need to plan the order in which to complete the steps. Use the activities below to help students become more effective planners.

❑ Use magazine pictures to show examples of problem situations. Show a picture to your students. Together, list at least three possible solutions. Then, discuss the solutions and choose the best one.

As you discuss the solutions, ask the students to name the resources needed for the solution. Students may list external resources such as money, a car or another person. They may also list internal resources such as talent, wisdom or patience.

❑ Play a game of problem solving with your students. Divide your students into groups and read them a common problem. Next, hand each group a note card with a list of four or five materials or resources that could be used for alternative solutions to the given problem. Then, have your students devise a solution using the items listed. Each group presents its list of items and solution to the class.

After discussing the alternative solutions, ask the class to plan the steps for the solution they think would be the most effective. Then, have your students decide how long each step would take and the best order in which to complete the steps.

Consider Other People

Name _____

Other people can often help you solve a problem. You must think about their *viewpoints* or reactions to the problem if you want their help.

Read the problem below. Then, read each viewpoint. Next, match the viewpoint with the person who might think that way by writing the correct letter in the blank. You may use a letter more than once.

Problem: Your brother had a car accident.

Viewpoints:

_____ 1. "Those young people just don't know how to handle a car."

_____ 2. "If my brother wrecked the car, how will I get to my dance lessons?"

_____ 3. "I knew I shouldn't have let him take the car."

_____ 4. "It was just an accident. I'm glad he's okay."

_____ 5. "Now Mom and Dad will never let me have the car."

_____ 6. "Is he all right? I'm sure it wasn't his fault."

_____ 7. "I was really scared when the police officer arrived."

_____ 8. "I hope he can still find a way to get to work."

_____ 9. "I wonder how long he'll be out of school."

_____ 10. "It wasn't his fault. The car came out of nowhere."

Persons:

a. you

b. Mom

c. passenger

d. sister

e. brother

f. grandparent

g. boss

h. teacher

i. friend

j. Dad

Parents' Viewpoints

When you have problems, you may need to ask your parents for advice or help. To make the most of your parents' help, consider their viewpoints and feelings.

Read the statements below describing parents' viewpoints. Think about how your parents usually react to problems. Then, write **Yes** or **No** in front of each statement to show how your parents might feel.

Example:

Yes   My parents think I am dependable.

_____   1. My dad likes to discuss problems.

_____   2. My mom and I can work out solutions together.

_____   3. My parents think I should solve my own problems.

_____   4. If Mom is upset, she can't listen very well.

_____   5. My parents don't want me to have a job.

_____   6. My dad sometimes cries when he's frustrated.

_____   7. When my mom gets home from work, she needs a few quiet minutes.

_____   8. My dad says, "Ask your mom," and Mom says, "Ask your dad."

_____   9. My parents don't like most of my friends.

_____   10. Mom loses her temper quickly.

Now, discuss your answers with your classmates. Discuss ways you could handle situations if you knew how your parents would react when you told them about the problems.

Best Time and Place

When you solve a problem, you need to choose the best time and place to talk to someone about it. Knowing where and when to talk to someone is important when you need the help of your family, friends, boss or teacher.

Read each problem, solution, and set of steps below. Then, circle **Yes** or **No** to indicate if the plan includes the best time and place. If not, suggest a better time and place.

1. Problem: You got an *F* on a science test.

   Solution: Tell my mother.

   Steps: After dinner, help my mother wash dishes in the kitchen. While helping, tell her about my grade.

   Is this the best time?   Yes   No   Is this the best place?   Yes   No

   When would be a better time or place? _____

2. Problem: Your friend is telling lies about you.

   Solution: Talk to her about the problem.

   Steps: Sit with her and her friends at lunch. Tell her what I heard and how upset I am.

   Is this the best time?   Yes   No   Is this the best place?   Yes   No

   When would be a better time or place? _____

3. Problem: You need to take a day off from work.

   Solution: Ask my boss for the day off.

   Steps: Go to my boss's office. While he is talking on the phone, ask for the day off.

   Is this the best time?   Yes   No   Is this the best place?   Yes   No

   When would be a better time or place? _____

84

Helping Hands

Asking for help from another person can be a wise move. Someone who sees your problem from another point of view may have good suggestions for solving a problem.

Read each problem below. In the blank before each problem, write the letters of people who could help you. Then, tell why you made the choices you did. You can use a letter more than once.

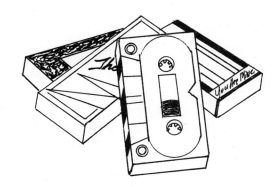

Problems:

1. You want to listen to your new cassettes, but your stereo speakers aren't working.

   Why did you choose this person? _____

   _____

2. You want a part-time job to earn money for a car.

   Why did you choose this person? _____

   _____

3. You hurt your arm in gym class. It still hurts after school.

   Why did you choose this person? _____

   _____

4. One of your friends isn't speaking to you and you don't know why.

   Why did you choose this person? _____

   _____

5. Your parents don't want you to get a job. They think it might make your grades drop.

   Why did you choose this person? _____

   _____

People:

a. Dad, who is a nurse

b. Mom, who likes to fix things

c. sister, who is a good cook and knows lots of people

d. brother, who works at a fast-food restaurant

e. friend, who is a good listener

f. Grandpa, who likes to help

g. friend, who has a job

ADDITIONAL ACTIVITIES

Solution plans often require other people's help, so your students need to be aware of how others think and feel. They also need to choose the best time and place to enlist the help of others. The activities below will enable your students to see others' viewpoints better.

- ❏ Arrange your students in a circle. Tell them to think of three people they know well. Next, have them select the most favorable time and place to ask these people for help. Then, share an example of a time when someone helped you successfully solve a problem. Discuss the time and place you asked for help. Encourage your students to share similar experiences.

- ❏ Read a problem and solution aloud. Have each student plan the steps for solving the problem. Then, ask the student to think of someone whose viewpoint or help would make the plan work more smoothly.

  Students may share their plans and the name of the person whose help they would seek. Encourage the other students to offer alternative ideas for who could help. Remind your students to consider others' viewpoints and needs.

Take Action!

Taking the first step can be the key to solving a problem successfully.

Read each problem below and the three possible first steps. Circle the letter of the step you think should be taken first. Then, explain your choice.

1. Problem: You took twice as much medicine as you should have.

    a. Call the doctor or pharmacist.

    b. Drink water.

    c. Look at the label for instructions.

    Why? _____

2. Problem: You are at the mall with your little sister, and she gets lost.

    a. Call her name.

    b. Call your parents.

    c. Ask the mall office for help.

    Why? _____

3. Problem: You delivered balloons to the wrong house.

    a. Take new balloons to the correct house.

    b. Tell my boss.

    c. Call the people who ordered the balloons and explain.

    Why? _____

4. Problem: You missed an important test in school.

    a. Go in early one morning to take the test.

    b. Talk to my teacher about a time to make up the test.

    c. Have my mother write an excuse for why I missed the test.

    Why? _____

Easy Does It

If your first step toward solving a problem is easy, the next steps will go smoothly. If the first step is too hard, you may never even begin to solve your problem.

Read these problems and solutions. Then, write the first step to take to solve the problems.

1. Problem: You need to lose 20 pounds.

    Solution: Go on a diet.

    First Step: _____

2. Problem: An older student is teasing you.

    Solution: Ignore her.

    First Step: _____

3. Problem: You've become more skilled at your job and you think you deserve more pay.

    Solution: Ask my boss for a raise.

    First Step: _____

4. Problem: You've moved to a new town and you don't know anyone.

    Solution: Go out and meet some people.

    First Step: _____

5. Problem: You don't think your parents will let you go to a party.

    Solution: Convince them to let me go.

    First Step: _____

Now, think of a problem you have. Then, decide what solution you'll use and what your first step will be.

    Problem: _____

    Solution: _____

    First Step: _____

88

Tell Someone

If you tell someone about the first step of your solution plan and when you'll do it, you're more likely to actually take the first step.

Read the problems and solutions below. Next, list your first step and when you would do it. Also, write who you would tell and how he could check on you.

Example:

Problem: The electricity goes off during a thunderstorm. You are alone. You hear a crash in the basement.

Solution: Find out what caused the noise.

First Step: *Get a flashlight and go to the basement.*

When? *Now*

Who could check and how? *Call a friend and have him call me back in five minutes.*

1. Problem: You need to earn money.

   Solution: Look for a job at a fast-food restaurant.

   First Step: _____

   When? _____

   Who could check and how? _____

2. Problem: You don't have enough money to buy the tennis shoes you want.

   Solution: Ask my parents to lend me the money.

   First Step: _____

   When? _____

   Who could check and how? _____

89

ADDITIONAL ACTIVITIES

Taking the first step in a solution plan can mean the difference between success and failure. Completing a fairly easy first step can give your students the motivation to complete the rest of the plan. Use the activities below to help your students practice taking the first step.

❑ Tell your students to write down two problems they would like to solve. Have them choose one problem and write a solution and a plan with three or more steps. Then, ask your students to share their plans with a classmate and discuss the first step and when they will do it. Encourage your students to devise a way for someone to check their progress and how they'll prove they took the first step. Later, talk about how important it is to set time lines for doing something and how some people need to be gently pushed to get going.

❑ Present a problem to your students. Have them share various first steps which could be part of a solution plan. Write several of these first steps on the board. Then, answer the following questions for each choice:

How easily could this be done?
Has it worked before?
Would it lead into the next step?
Could you do it on your own?

After discussion, decide as a group which would be the best first step.

RESULTS

Goal: To predict outcomes and examine results.

OBJECTIVES

PREDICTING OUTCOMES: To predict possible results when given problems, solutions, and plans.

EXAMINING RESULTS: To evaluate results and generate alternative solutions and plans when needed.

This section of *Problem Solving for Teens* contains exercises for your students to predict the possible results of plans and to analyze those results. The exercises will help them recognize that a plan can be altered or improved if it doesn't work the first time.

TEACHING SUGGESTIONS

1. Review the definition of *results*. Results are outcomes that occur when the solution plan is put into action. Then, discuss the value of examining results to decide if the plan was successful, if it needs revision, or if a new plan is the best option.

2. Teach your students to examine their plans and consider all the possible outcomes and potential problems. Provide examples of predictions that have been helpful to you. For instance, when you prepared for an interview for a job, you may have tried to predict what questions would be asked at the interview.

    Encourage your students to consider what they know about other persons involved in the plan and how these persons react at different times and places. Describe various situations and have your students predict how a parent, friend, or boss would react. Then, your students can discuss their answers in small groups.

3. Help your students see how results can be evaluated while they're happening. Sometimes, minor changes at the last minute can make a difference. Discuss television shows and movies in which last minute changes have taken place. A classic example takes place in the movie *The Wizard of Oz* when Dorothy and her friends discover that the wizard is just a man behind a curtain. When they discover that the wizard is just a man, they have to quickly change their plan. Ask your students for examples from their own lives.

    Discuss the value of having an alternative or *backup* plan. Give examples of how the quick implementation of a backup plan can lead to the desired results.

    As your students examine results, practice determining if a result is good or bad. Usually, the result is good if the desired solution is achieved. The result is considered bad if the problem isn't solved or if a problem occurs that changes the outcome. Talk about accepting responsibility for the results, whether they're good or bad. Students can learn to recognize that the results are often consequences of their plans.

4. Cite major mistakes that famous people have made and tell how they learned from those experiences. For example, name several famous athletes who used drugs to help solve problems and subsequently had to undergo treatment. Then, share how you have learned to handle mistakes through your own experiences. You may want to tell about an incident from your teenage years involving your parents, friends, teachers, or a boss. Your students may also share mistakes they've made if they feel comfortable doing so.

5. To help build your students' self-confidence, discuss some ways they can reward themselves for positive results of their problem solving. For example, they may tell someone about the results, purchase a treat, or accept praise.

What Is a Result?

A result is what happens when you carry out your solution plan.

Read each problem and solution. Then, read each sentence below the solution. Circle **Yes** if the sentence describes a result or **No** if it does not.

Example:

    Problem: Paint is peeling off the garage.

    Solution: Dad will repaint the garage.

    a.   The freshly painted garage looks great.   (Yes)   No

    b.   The gutters also need to be repaired.   Yes   (No)

1.   Problem: You forgot to send a birthday card to your grandmother.

    Solution: Call her on the telephone and apologize.

    a.   Grandma sends me a gift on my birthday.   Yes   No

    b.   Grandma understands and says it's okay.   Yes   No

2.   Problem: Your parents think you play your stereo too loudly.

    Solution: Close my bedroom door and wear headphones when I play my stereo.

    a.   My parents ask to borrow the headphones.   Yes   No

    b.   My parents thank me.   Yes   No

3.   Problem: Your boss is upset because you came to work late twice.

    Solution: Leave home sooner to get to work.

    a.   My boss praises me for being on time.   Yes   No

    b.   I buy a new watch.   Yes   No

4.   Problem: You don't understand your math assignment.

    Solution: Ask the math teacher for help.

    a.   My best friend also asks the teacher for help.   Yes   No

    b.   I get a good grade on the assignment.   Yes   No

The Results Are In

When you carry out your solution plan, you'll be rewarded with good results.

Read each problem and solution. Then, describe a possible result of each situation.

Example:

    Problem: You're mowing the lawn when the mower runs out of gas.

    Solution: I push the mower to the shed and fill it up with gas.

    Result: *I can finish mowing the lawn.* _____

1.   Problem: You lose your new winter gloves at school.

    Solution: I look in the "Lost and Found" box at school.

    Result: _____

2.   Problem: There's only one piece of pie left and both you and your brother want it.

    Solution: Cut the piece of pie in half.

    Result: _____

3.   Problem: You have a date on Friday and find out you're supposed to work.

    Solution: I ask someone to trade hours with me, with my boss's permission.

    Result: _____

4.   Problem: You miss your friend who recently moved to a different state.

    Solution: I write her a long letter.

    Result: _____

5.   Problem: Your parents come home after being gone for three days. The house is very messy and your parents blame you.

    Solution: Explain that I didn't have time to clean up after my brother and sister, but that I tried to keep my things neat.

    Result: _____

Other People Count

Name _____

To predict outcomes more accurately, you need to know how other people in the solution plan might react.

Read each problem and solution below. Then, answer the questions.

Example:

Problem: You want to stay out later at night.

Solution: Convince my parents to let me have a later curfew.

When is the best time to talk to your parents?   *at dinnertime* _____

Who could help you convince your parents?   *my older brother* _____

1. Problem: You want to go to a baseball game this weekend, but you have to work.

Solution: Ask my boss if someone else can work this weekend.

When is the best time to ask your boss? _____

Who could work for you? _____

2. Problem: You want to use the car on Friday night.

Solution: Ask Dad if I can use the car.

When is the best time to ask Dad? _____

Who could help you convince your dad? _____

3. Problem: You failed a science test.

Solution: Ask the teacher if I can retake the test.

When is the best time to ask the teacher? _____

Who could help you study for the test? _____

4. Problem: You don't know how to dance.

Solution: Find someone to teach me how to dance.

Who could teach you? _____

When could this person teach you? _____

Success or Failure

When you have several solution plans to choose from, you can predict more accurately which one will work better.

Read each problem and solution below. Then, read the three possible plans. Rate each plan by putting an **X** before a plan you think will work. Put an **O** before a plan you think might not work. Put a **?** if you're not sure.

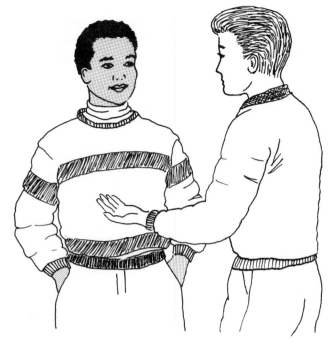

1. Problem: You forgot your lunch money.

    Solution: Borrow money from someone.

    Plans:

    _____ a. Ask my best friend if I can borrow lunch money.

    _____ b. Ask a stranger for lunch money.

    _____ c. Ask my math teacher for lunch money and promise to do all my homework.

2. Problem: You lost your wallet.

    Solution: Look for it.

    Plans:

    _____ a. Tell my friend and my mom to look for it.

    _____ b. Look in the last classroom I was in and in my locker.

    _____ c. Check with my friends and teachers, retrace my day's steps, and look in the "Lost and Found" box.

3. Problem: Your parents want you to stay home and babysit your brother, but you want to go to a party.

    Solution: Convince my parents to let me go to the party.

    Plans:

    _____ a. Start a loud argument with my parents.

    _____ b. Tell my parents I will stay home the next time they want me to babysit.

    _____ c. Offer to find another babysitter and to pay him.

Be Ready for Anything

Name _____

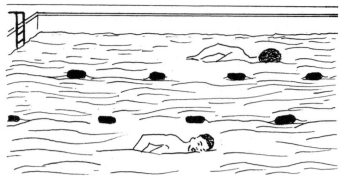

You won't always know if your plan is going to turn out the way you want it to. There are many things that can change the outcome.

Read the items below. Then, list three possible outcomes or results.

1. Problem: You want to win a race at your first swim meet.

   Solution: Practice a lot and be ready for the meet.

   Plan: Practice every day, get plenty of rest, and eat the right foods.

   Possible Outcomes:

   a. _____

   b. _____

   c. _____

2. Problem: Your brother gets teased every day after school.

   Solution: Talk to the people who are teasing him.

   Plan: Explain to each person how my brother feels, and ask each person to stop teasing him.

   Possible Outcomes:

   a. _____

   b. _____

   c. _____

Now, write down a problem you will face in the future or have right now. Choose a solution and plan to solve the problem. Then, list three possible outcomes.

   Problem: _____

   Solution: _____

   Plan: _____

   Possible Outcomes:

   a. _____

   b. _____

   c. _____

Last Minute Changes

Sometimes things happen at the last minute to change a situation. Then, you need to quickly change your solution plan.

Read each situation below. Then, tell what the result might be for two different solution plans.

1. Problem: During your senior year, your family is moving to a different city.

    Solution: Move with your family and make the best of it.

    At the last minute: Your football team is doing really well and you have been named one of the most valuable players.

    Plan A: Wish your team well and move with your family.

    Result: _____

    Plan B: Move in with a friend's family and finish the school year.

    Result: _____

2. Problem: You want to buy an expensive shirt, but you don't have enough money.

    Solution: Borrow the extra money from your dad so you can buy it.

    At the last minute: The shirt goes on sale.

    Plan A: Buy the shirt and a belt since your dad loaned you the money.

    Result: _____

    Plan B: Buy the shirt with your own money and return your dad's money.

    Result: _____

3. Problem: A friend needs someone to work for her tonight.

    Solution: You will work for her.

    At the last minute: Another friend calls you and asks you to go with her to a concert.

    Plan A: Call the first friend and tell her you can't work for her after all.

    Result: _____

    Plan B: Tell the second friend you can't go to the concert.

    Result: _____

ADDITIONAL ACTIVITIES

Your students need lots of practice in predicting possible outcomes of solution plans. When predicting outcomes, they also need to realize that people solve problems in different ways. Use the activities below to help your students better predict the results of plans.

❑ Play a game of *I Predict*. Prepare cards with problems on them and the steps needed to solve the problems. Include possible results for the situations, too. The problems may include things like cleaning the bathroom, researching something for school, learning how to take someone's order, or changing a light bulb.

Have a student choose a card and role-play the first two or three steps of the plan. Ask another student to role-play his predicted result. Then, compare the role-played result to the one listed on the card. Ask another student to role-play an alternative result. Discuss how changes can occur at the last minute.

As a variation, have students prepare cards with problems and plans of action for role-playing. Have the students act out one of their own problems. Then, they can ask someone to predict what plan is on the card and to act out that plan. Encourage the students to compare the plans to help increase their awareness that not everyone solves plans in the same way.

❑ To give your students practice in predicting outcomes, ask them to write about a fictitious character who has a day filled with problems. Then, have them list one of the problems, the solution, the plan of action, and the expected result. Have the students share their examples without disclosing the expected results. The other students can predict possible outcomes. The students can then compare these outcomes with their own. Again, call attention to individual differences in plans and results.

Who's Responsible?

When several people are involved in a problem situation, someone may need to be responsible for the results.

Read about each situation below. Then, decide who caused the results and write your answer on the line.

1. You were driving the car during driver's education training. Your friend was laughing in the back seat. Even though your teacher said never to turn around while driving, you turned around to see what was so funny. You bumped into the car in front of you at the stoplight.

   Who caused these results? _____

2. You were making popcorn in the kitchen. Your sister told you that you had put in too much popcorn. Your mom walked in as popcorn overflowed from the popper.

   Who caused these results? _____

3. Every day, your mom fed food from the table to your overweight dog. You took the dog for a walk every day after school. When you took the dog to the vet, she said the dog had heart trouble due to its extra weight.

   Who caused these results? _____

4. You work at a fast-food restaurant. One day, you were taking and filling orders at the drive-up window. Several people complained that you gave them the wrong orders.

   Who caused these results? _____

5. While you were at the shoe store, you tried on a pair of shoes in the latest style. The salesclerk told you the shoes looked great, so you bought them. The first time you wore the shoes, you discovered that they were too tight.

   Who caused these results? _____

6. Your friend asked you to go to the beach with her. You stayed at the beach for three hours. When you got home, you had a painful sunburn.

   Who caused these results? _____

7. You didn't finish your English homework, so the teacher made you stay after school to finish it. You missed a ride home with your friend and had to walk home in the rain.

   Who caused these results? _____

100

Good News, Bad News

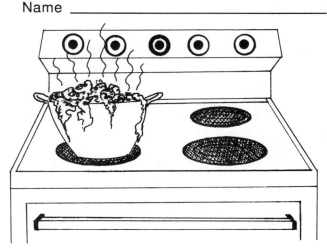

Sometimes you need to watch the results of your plan as they're happening. You can then decide whether or not to change your plan.

Read the items below. Circle **Good** or **Bad** to tell what kind of results you think you'll get. Next, circle **Yes** or **No** to tell if you would change your plan.

1. While you're fixing dinner, a friend calls you. You talk on the phone for 15 minutes.

   What will the results be for your dinner?   Good   Bad

   Would you change your plan after you got off the phone?   Yes   No

2. While you're trying to convince your parents to let you go to a party, your brother breaks a lamp.

   What will the results be for convincing your parents?   Good   Bad

   Would you change your plan after the lamp broke?   Yes   No

3. While you're trying to fix your bike, your brother comes home. He's really good at fixing things.

   What will the results be for fixing your bike?   Good   Bad

   Would you change your plan after your brother got home?   Yes   No

4. While you're at a job interview, your neighbor tells the person interviewing you that you're a good worker.

   What will the results be for your interview?   Good   Bad

   Would you change your plan after your neighbor left?   Yes   No

5. While you're giving a speech in English class, you begin coughing and can't stop.

   What will the results be for your speech?   Good   Bad

   Would you change your plan while you were giving your speech? Yes   No

6. As you're heading out the door to go to work, you see a car accident. You go to help the people involved.

   What will the results be for getting to work on time?   Good   Bad

   Would you change your plan after you helped the people?   Yes   No

Check It Out!

Name _____

Sometimes you have to wait to find out the results of your plan. You may even need help from someone to find out the results.

There are many ways you can check results. Read about the different ways listed below.

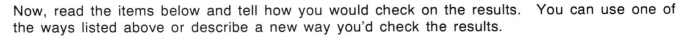

- ❏ Call someone to find out what happened.

- ❏ Go to see for yourself.

- ❏ Write a letter and ask what happened.

- ❏ Ask a friend who was part of the plan to tell you what happened.

- ❏ Have someone take a photograph or videotape the results.

Now, read the items below and tell how you would check on the results. You can use one of the ways listed above or describe a new way you'd check the results.

1. You wrote a letter to apply for a job.

   _____

2. You asked a friend to find out if the person you want to date is dating anyone.

   _____

3. You played a joke on the teacher and then left the room.

   _____

4. You left your dad a message on the answering machine to say you would be an hour late for dinner.

   _____

5. You took a very hard English test.

   _____

6. You dropped off a birthday present at a friend's house because you couldn't make it to her birthday party.

   _____

7. You asked your boss for a day of vacation.

   _____

Have a Backup Plan

Name _____

If your first solution plan doesn't work, it's a good idea to have a backup plan you can use quickly.

Read the items below. Then, circle **Good** or **Bad** to show what the results were. If you circle **Bad**, list a backup plan you could use.

1. Problem: You don't get enough allowance.

    Solution: Try to earn more money.

    Plan: Ask your neighbors if they need their lawns mowed.

    Result: None of your neighbors needs his lawn mowed.

    Were the results good or bad?   Good   Bad

    If the results were bad, give a backup plan. _____

    _____

2. Problem: The teacher assigns two pages of math problems for tomorrow, and you don't have time to do the assignment tonight.

    Solution: Find some free time during the day to do the assignment.

    Plan: Do the assignment during a study hall period.

    Result: Your friend talks to you during most of the study hall period and you don't finish the assignment.

    Were the results good or bad?   Good   Bad

    If the results were bad, give a backup plan. _____

    _____

3. Problem: You forget to give your mom telephone messages.

    Solution: Write down your mom's telephone messages.

    Plan: Keep paper and pencil by the telephone.

    Result: You took good messages and gave them to Mom.

    Were the results good or bad?   Good   Bad

    If the results were bad, give a backup plan. _____

Learning from Mistakes

Name _____

You can learn from the mistakes you make as you try to solve problems. What you learn can help you the next time you solve a problem.

Read each situation below. Then, tell what you could learn from that situation.

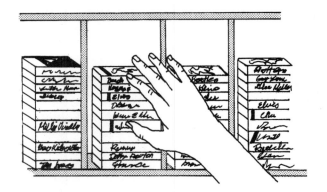

1. You lose your friend's cassette tape. You decide to steal a new one, but you get caught.

    What could you learn?

    _____

2. You yell at your dad about curfew rules. He grounds you for two weeks.

    What could you learn?

    _____

3. You invite several friends to your neighbors' home while you are babysitting. Your friends are still there when the child's parents come home.

    What could you learn?

    _____

4. Your parents won't let you drive the family car. While they are out of town, you take the car to a party and the paint gets scratched.

    What could you learn?

    _____

5. A new student tries to introduce herself to you, but you walk away because you are very shy. Now, she avoids you when she sees you.

    What could you learn?

    _____

6. It's time to leave for work, but your work uniform is dirty.

    What could you learn?

    _____

104

Nice Job!

Name _____

If your solution leads to good results, you deserve a reward.   A reward can help you feel good about yourself.

Read the list of rewards below.   Then, place a check mark on the line before each reward you would like.

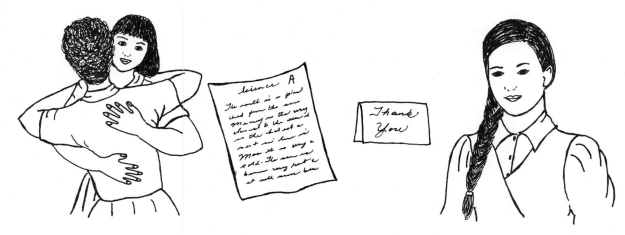

_____ 1. a smile	_____ 13. a word of praise
_____ 2. a good grade	_____ 14. renting a videotape
_____ 3. a *Thank You* card	_____ 15. use of the car
_____ 4. a hug	_____ 16. watching TV
_____ 5. pizza	_____ 17. having a friend over
_____ 6. money	_____ 18. staying up late
_____ 7. new clothing	_____ 19. sleeping late
_____ 8. free time	_____ 20. no homework
_____ 9. a handshake	_____ 21. going to a movie
_____ 10. a pat on the back	_____ 22. candy
_____ 11. time to use the computer	_____ 23. going to a friend's house
_____ 12. a new cassette tape	_____ 24. a trip to the mall

Now, list four other rewards you would like.

_____

_____

_____

_____

What's the Reward?

The kind of reward you get depends on the situation. For example, you'd probably get different rewards for getting all *As* than for getting an *A* in one class.

Read each situation below. Then, tell what a good reward would be for solving each problem.

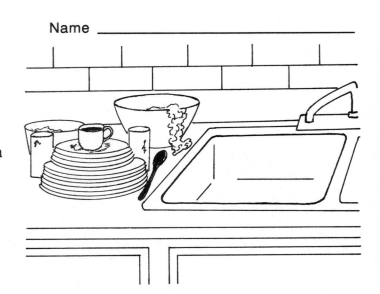

Example:

    Problem: The home where you're babysitting has lots of dirty dishes.

    Solution: Do the dishes.

    Reward: *The parents give you extra money for doing the dishes.*

1.   Problem: You have a science test next week and you don't understand the material.

    Solution: Study with a friend who understands the material.

    Reward: _____

2.   Problem: Your brother needs a ride home after soccer practice.

    Solution: Offer to pick up your brother.

    Reward: _____

3.   Problem: Your best friend broke her leg and won't be back in school for a week.

    Solution: Send her a bouquet of flowers.

    Reward: _____

4.   Problem: You accidentally gave a customer the wrong change.

    Solution: Apologize to the customer and give him the correct change.

    Reward: _____

5.   Problem: You have a fever and an upset stomach on a school day.

    Solution: Take some medicine, stay home, and rest.

    Reward: _____

ADDITIONAL ACTIVITIES

Being able to predict results or outcomes is a critical skill for your students. As results occur, students need to be able to examine them and decide if the plan needs to be revised or if they need to use a backup plan. Judging if a result is good or bad also takes much practice. To help your students acquire these skills, use the activities below.

❑ Make up four sets of cards to be used in a circle game. Write one of the following problem-solving steps on each card: *solution*, *plan*, *result*, and *alternative*. Give each student a set of the four cards.

State a problem. Have the first student give a solution to the problem. If you think she gives a good solution, she gives the *solution* card back to you. If she doesn't give a good solution, the next person in the circle gets a chance. Continue this process until someone gives an appropriate solution. Repeat this process for the *plan* and *result* steps. After the *result* step, the next student judges whether the result was good or bad. If the result was bad, that student has ten seconds to propose an alternate plan. If he does so, he gives the *alternative* card back to you. Play continues until one student has given all of her cards back to you. That student is the winner.

❑ As your students examine results, discuss how a good result may have been achieved through a questionable method. Have your students role-play situations in which the problem appears to have been solved, but the plan they used raises problems. Pose problem situations like *Your friend is being teased and you plan to beat up the teaser* or *You need a new pair of earrings, so you plan to steal a pair*. Ask the students to offer their opinions on whether the problem would really be solved by taking these actions, and to generate better alternative plans.

❑ Discuss examples of how you may need to solve small problems on your way to solving a larger problem. For example, a person who needs to lose 50 pounds may set goals of losing ten pounds at a time. In this situation, each goal leads to the eventual solution of the problem. Another example could involve several small goals being met on the way to totally remodeling a room. Have your students discuss why it's important to examine the results of each step in order to achieve the larger goal. Encourage them to talk about what they could do if they weren't getting the results they wanted along the way.

PREVENTING PROBLEMS

Goal: To recognize possible problems and prevent them from occurring.

OBJECTIVES

RECOGNIZING WARNING SIGNS: To identify early signs of possible problems.

LEARNING FROM THE PAST: To apply knowledge of past problems to prevent similar future problems.

CHOOSING PREVENTION METHODS: To generate several ways to prevent a problem and choose the best method.

This section of *Problem Solving for Teens* contains exercises for your students to practice recognizing signs of possible problems and to apply information gained from previous situations to prevent future difficulties. The exercises will help your students discover acceptable ways to prevent problems. Through follow-up discussions, you can help your students select the best ways to prevent problems.

TEACHING SUGGESTIONS

1. Before beginning the exercises, discuss the meaning of *prevention*. Prevention involves doing something ahead of time to keep certain events from happening. Help students learn that it's best to try to prevent a problem before it occurs.

2. Ask your students to offer specific ways preventing problems could be beneficial to them, such as saving time and money, conserving energy, and keeping people happy. Share an event from your own life that illustrates one of these benefits. Then, ask students to share personal examples.

3. Review the concepts from Unit 1 concerning warning signs of possible problems. Emphasize that you are looking for very early signs that can keep problems from ever happening. Begin by focusing on concrete visual warning signs. Help your students list signs that can be seen, such as the oil light on a car or broken glass on the floor. Discuss the possible problem indicated by each sign.

   Then, role-play the more subtle facial expressions and nonverbal indicators used as warning signs, such as a frown, clenched fists, or fingers tapping on a desk. Explain how being aware of other people's moods can also enable your students to prevent problems.

4. Encourage your students to look for similarities between past and future problems. Describe a past problem and a future problem. Then, ask students to tell how the problems are alike. For example, tell about a time your older brother dented the family car and relate it to a time in the future when you may get a speeding ticket. Another example would be to tell about being teased because of large ears and ask how that could be similar to being called names.

5. Group problems into four categories: home, school, friends, and work. Divide problems the students have had in the past into these categories. Your list may look like this:

   Home   disagreements with sisters and brothers, trouble dealing with parents, failure to follow rules or do assigned jobs

   School   problems with a teacher, difficulty with homework and tests, misbehavior in the classroom

   Friends   jealousy, dishonesty, loss of trust, arguments, unpopularity

   Work   problems with the boss, being unable to work with fellow employees

6. As you discuss the past problems of your students, ask the following questions:

   1. Did anyone try a solution because it had worked before?

   2. Did anyone solve a problem the same way a friend had?

   3. Are there any solutions that have worked more than once for similar problems?

   4. Were your students aware they had been involved in a problem like this before?

7. Discuss common ways your students can prevent problems, such as walking away, communicating, and getting help right away. Ask what methods have worked best for your students.

   Help your students recognize whether or not a problem can be prevented. Describe problem situations and ask if they could be prevented. For the problems which could be prevented, ask students to generate several ways to do so. Then, have them choose the best one or two methods to use and justify their choices.

Prevent or Ignore?

If you prevent something, you keep it from happening. If you ignore something, you pretend to not know about something that's already happened.

Read each situation below. Then, circle the correct words to tell if you can prevent a problem or if it's too late. Next, write what might happen if you ignore the situation.

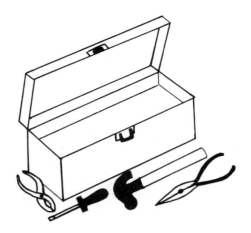

1. You borrowed your dad's tools without asking him, and you lost his wrench.

     can prevent a problem   too late

     What might happen if you ignore the situation? _____

     _____

2. You talked back to your teacher, and she sent you to the principal's office.

     can prevent a problem   too late

     What might happen if you ignore the situation? _____

     _____

3. You're driving and someone 20 feet in front of you just slammed on her brakes.

     can prevent a problem   too late

     What might happen if you ignore the situation? _____

     _____

4. A student in the lunchroom called you a name, and you want to hit him.

     can prevent a problem   too late

     What might happen if you ignore the situation? _____

     _____

5. You don't want to sweep the floor, but your boss says you have to. You want to argue with her.

     can prevent a problem   too late

     What might happen if you ignore the situation? _____

     _____

Plan Ahead

Solving problems can take a lot of time, money, and energy. Planning ahead and preventing problems can help you save time, money, and energy.

Read each problem below. Put a check mark in front of each thing you could have saved by preventing the problem. Then, list another benefit of preventing this problem.

Example:

You ruined the sweater you borrowed from your friend.

_____ time ___✔___ money _____ energy

Another benefit: *My friend wouldn't be upset.* _____

1. You were suspended from school for fighting.

_____ time _____ money _____ energy

Another benefit: _____

2. You forgot your lunch at home.

_____ time _____ money _____ energy

Another benefit: _____

3. You missed the bus because you were talking with a friend too long.

_____ time _____ money _____ energy

Another benefit: _____

4. You don't have any money because you spent all of your allowance.

_____ time _____ money _____ energy

Another benefit: _____

5. You failed a history test because you didn't study.

_____ time _____ money _____ energy

Another benefit: _____

Early Warning Signs

Name _____

Sometimes there are early warning signs of a problem. If you're aware of these signs, you might prevent the problem from happening.

Read each situation below. Write the possible problem on the line. Then, list the early warning signs that point to this possible problem.

1. The oil light on your 14-year-old family car has been on for two months. The car is hard to start and the brakes squeak. Now, the car won't start.

   Possible problem: _____

   Early signs: _____

   _____

   _____

2. Your mom is very tired when she gets home from work. Dinner isn't ready and the house is messy. Mom is an impatient person who doesn't like a messy house.

   Possible problem: _____

   Early signs: _____

   _____

   _____

3. You have a strict teacher who won't accept late homework. You forgot to do your assignment for the third time this week. The teacher was angry with you the last two times you forgot.

   Possible problem: _____

   Early signs: _____

   _____

   _____

Warning signs help you see when problems are about to happen. Discuss how these problems could be prevented.

Earliest Warning Signs

Name _____

Some warning signs appear earlier than others. In order to prevent most problems, you need to notice the first or earliest signs.

Read each warning sign below. Then, think about what may have been an earlier warning sign, and write it on the line.

Example:

Your houseplants are wilting and turning brown.

Earlier sign: *The soil was dry.* _____

1. You got an *F* in science on your report card.

   Earlier sign: _____

2. When you pushed down the toaster handle, sparks came out.

   Earlier sign: _____

3. You have a cold.

   Earlier sign: _____

4. The only person you've been dating wants to date other people.

   Earlier sign: _____

5. Your boss warns you not to leave work early again.

   Earlier sign: _____

6. Your car seat has a large rip in it.

   Earlier sign: _____

7. Your best friend doesn't invite you to her birthday party.

   Earlier sign: _____

8. Your car runs out of gas.

   Earlier sign: _____

9. Your parents ground you for two weeks for not doing your weekly jobs.

   Earlier sign: _____

Predict Problems

Name _____

If you notice early warning signs, you can often predict possible problems. That gives you the best chance of preventing the problems.

Read each situation and list of early signs below. Next, predict a possible problem and tell how you might prevent that problem.

Example:

    Situation: You walk into a beauty salon without an appointment, hoping to get a haircut.

    Early Signs: busy workers, crowded waiting room

    Possible problem: *It will take a long time to get a haircut.*

    How to prevent the problem: *Call ahead to get an appointment.*

1.   Situation: Your mom knocks on your door and says you need to get up.

    Early Signs: Mom's tone of voice, your alarm clock didn't go off

    Possible problem: _____

    How to prevent the problem: _____

2.   Situation: Your car keeps veering to the side of the road.

    Early Signs: low air pressure in one tire, car doesn't seem level

    Possible problem: _____

    How to prevent the problem: _____

3.   Situation: You come home from vacation and your stereo is missing.

    Early signs: broken window, open front door

    Possible problem: _____

    How to prevent the problem: _____

4.   Situation: The teacher called you up to his desk.

    Early Signs: several late assignments, an *F* on a test

    Possible problem: _____

    How to prevent the problem: _____

ADDITIONAL ACTIVITIES

Students need to recognize early warning signs of possible problems. Then, they can try to predict the problems that may occur and prevent them. Use the activities below to help your students better identify warning signs and problems which can be prevented.

☐ Do an activity called *Watch Your Time*. Read a possible problem to a student. Some possible problems may be: you and your friend disagree about where to go for pizza, you keep making mistakes at work, your school locker is a mess, or your parents don't like the way you want to get your hair cut. Have the student decide at what point the problem can be prevented and at what point it needs to be solved. Have the other students indicate agreement or disagreement, and explain their reasoning.

☐ Describe a problem and ask three students to give early warning signs that could have signaled that problem. Have a fourth student decide which sign would have happened first, second, and third. He can also list additional warning signs. You may want to begin by using concrete problems which include objects that may break or become worn, such as clothing items, appliances, cars, televisions, stereos, or computers.

☐ Have one of your students imagine he is at a given location, such as at a football game. Have the student identify a problem that might occur at this location. Have the next student list possible warning signs of this problem and tell if the problem could be prevented. Other possible locations could be: a rock and roll concert, a restaurant, a department store, a school classroom, a home setting, or a friend's house.

Gaining Experience

Name _____

You gain problem-solving experience by remembering what you or others have done in the past. An idea that worked well then may help prevent or solve a similar problem now.

Read each problem below. Then, read the three past problems listed. Circle the letter of the past problem that might help you know what to do for this problem.

1. You are sent to the principal's office because you hit someone.

   a. You once were caught trying to steal something.

   b. You were grounded for getting home late.

   c. You were in the principal's office for being tardy several times.

2. Other students are teasing you about your weight problem.

   a. Your dad was angry with you because you got your ear pierced.

   b. People made fun of your new haircut last week.

   c. Your friend has very crooked teeth.

3. You don't know if your parents will let you go to a party which lasts until 1:00 A.M. Your friends are going.

   a. You asked your parents to raise your allowance to what your friends get.

   b. Your mom was upset when you didn't practice the piano.

   c. Your sister was angry because you took her clothes without asking.

4. You are nervous about a job interview.

   a. Your friend was fired for doing poor work.

   b. You remember when your mom applied for a job.

   c. You lost an important homework assignment.

Compare your answers with others. Tell how you think the experience of the past problem could help prevent or solve the present problem.

Making a Connection

Name _____

Can you tell which problems are alike? If you can make a connection between a past and a future problem, you can often prevent problems.

Read the problems below. Match the problems which have something in common by writing the letter in the blank. Remember, your ideas may be different than someone else's ideas.

_____ 1. You had a tooth filled.

_____ 2. You talked back to a teacher.

_____ 3. You are shy around strangers.

_____ 4. Math was hard for you.

_____ 5. You backed into another car.

_____ 6. You ruined your mom's golf club.

_____ 7. You can't run very fast.

_____ 8. You were late for work.

_____ 9. You made a long-distance phone call and got a wrong number.

_____ 10. You were afraid of the dark.

_____ 11. You forgot how to get to the dentist's office.

_____ 12. You lost your work badge.

_____ a. You ruined your sister's sweater.

_____ b. You hate to get up in front of people.

_____ c. You can't hit a baseball very well.

_____ d. You need help making a phone call to another country.

_____ e. You have a toothache.

_____ f. You take the wrong road on the way to a friend's house.

_____ g. You need help with your science homework.

_____ h. You are afraid of dogs.

_____ i. You lose your time card at work.

_____ j. You are late for school.

_____ k. You told your mom, "No way!"

_____ l. Someone ran into your parents' car when you were driving.

Compare your answers with your classmates. Discuss how experience with a past problem in the left column could help you prevent or handle the similar problem in the right column.

Handling Future Problems

Name _____

It's helpful to remember what you learn when you solve a problem so you can handle future problems better.

Read each situation below. Tell what you could have learned from solving the problem and what you could do to prevent a similar problem in the future.

Example:

You had trouble doing your science homework, so you didn't finish it. You failed the assignment.

What you learned: _You fail if you don't do the homework._

Preventing a future problem: _Ask for help on hard assignments._

1. Your car wouldn't start after school, so you called your brother to ask him for a ride home.

   What you learned: _____

   Preventing a future problem: _____

2. You were supposed to work the night of a party. You didn't go to work because you didn't want to, so you were fired.

   What you learned: _____

   Preventing a future problem: _____

3. You got home from a date an hour later than you were supposed to. Your parents grounded you for a week.

   What you learned: _____

   Preventing a future problem: _____

4. You were jealous of your friend's new car, so you told lies about her. Then, she wouldn't talk to you.

   What you learned: _____

   Preventing a future problem: _____

5. When you made the French fries at work, you put too much salt on them. Your boss was upset with you because customers returned their salty French fries.

   What you learned: _____

   Preventing a future problem: _____

119

ADDITIONAL ACTIVITIES

Drawing associations between situations is a crucial and difficult skill to learn. Your students need to use what they have learned from past problems to improve their ability to handle future problems. The activities below will help your students make the connection between past and future problems.

❑ Have your students work in pairs. Give them the categories of home, school, friends, and work. Ask them to list similar problems they have encountered in each category. Then, have them work together to answer these questions:

How are the problems alike?

How did each person handle these problems?

Were any of the solutions similar?

What did you learn from these problems?

As a class, discuss the answers to the questions. Have the students tell how to use what was learned to prevent similar problems in the future.

❑ Show the students a group of five typical teenage problems. Ask them to list personal situations that are similar to those you wrote. They may also list similar problems other teenagers have had. Have three students offer both good and bad ideas for solutions. Help the students discover how this information can help prevent future problems.

❑ Draw a time line with *past*, *present*, and *future* on the chalkboard. Give the students a list of problems, indicating whether the problems are past, present, or future. Then, have the students describe related problems which are examples of the two missing types. For instance, if a problem is listed as being in the past, the students can describe similar present and future problems. Again, help your students draw associations between the various situations.

```
   Past              Present           Future

<------------------|-----------------|----------------->
                   |                 |
                   |                 |
```

Try Prevention

Preventing a problem can be done in many ways. You need to choose the way you think will work best and then try it.

Read the problems below. Then, match each problem to one or more ways it could be prevented by writing a letter or letters in the blank. There may be more than one good way to prevent each problem. Remember, your ideas may be different than someone else's ideas. Share your answers with someone.

Problems:

Ways to prevent problems:

_____ Your parents think you talk on the phone too much.

_____ Someone teased you about the shape of your nose.

_____ You're tired of being blamed for things your sister does.

_____ Your friend is drunk and wants to drive home.

_____ Your boyfriend thinks you have been secretly dating others.

_____ You feel like your boss favors another worker.

_____ The seam of your pants looks like it's ready to tear.

_____ You're having trouble doing your math homework by yourself.

_____ You keep giving the wrong change at work.

_____ Your brother says mean things about your best friend.

A. Walk away.

B. Talk about it right away to clear up any misunderstandings.

C. Set a time to talk about it later.

D. Don't make a big deal out of it.

E. Ask for help.

F. Get help from someone before a problem occurs.

G. Stay away from a person or situation where the problem occurs.

Now, tell about two other good ways to prevent problems. Discuss these ways with someone in your class.

Talk About It

Talking can help other people understand what you do. Sometimes, others don't know how you feel or why you act the way you do.

Read each situation below. Write **Yes** or **No** to tell if talking about the problem could help prevent possible problems.

_____ 1. Your dad thinks you spent all your allowance. You have been giving it to a friend who doesn't have any lunch money.

_____ 2. Your teacher is upset because you haven't turned in homework twice this week. He doesn't know that your mom is in the hospital.

_____ 3. You dropped your plate of food on the floor and you had to clean it up.

_____ 4. Your boss wants you to come to work earlier. She doesn't know you have to take a bus and you can't get there sooner.

_____ 5. Your brother is mad because you borrowed his tapes and left them lying all over the car.

_____ 6. The school counselor doesn't know why you don't pay attention in class and don't do your homework.

_____ 7. When you went hiking with a friend, you fell and broke your ankle.

_____ 8. Your parents found out you skipped school today.

_____ 9. You don't eat much dinner at your friend's house. Her family doesn't know you are allergic to wheat and milk.

_____ 10. Your teacher expects you to type a report on the computer. You just moved to this school and have never used a computer.

_____ 11. You don't like today's school lunch, so you skip lunch.

_____ 12. You're late for a job interview. You weren't able to call and explain that you were going to be late because you had a flat tire.

_____ 13. While you're at work, you start to feel sick. Your boss is upset because you aren't work fast enough.

_____ 14. You're trying on a shirt in a clothing store. The shirt is too small.

122

Choose Your Method

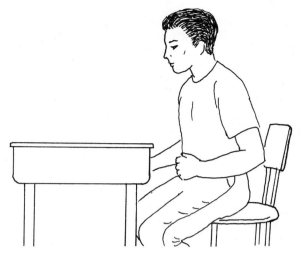

When you're facing a possible problem, choose the prevention method you think will work the best.

Read each situation below. Tell what you would do to try to prevent a possible problem, and explain why you would take that action.

Example:

You have an upset stomach during class.

I would   *ask the teacher if I could go see the nurse.* _____

Why?   *I could get help before my stomach started to feel worse.* _____

1. An older student is making fun of the way you dress.

    I would _____

    Why? _____

2. Someone steps in front of you in the checkout line at the grocery store.

    I would _____

    Why? _____

3. You're not sure if you're on the right bus.

    I would _____

    Why? _____

4. You carpool to work with Dean and Bill. Whenever Bill drives, you're late.

    I would _____

    Why? _____

5. You and your sister don't like to watch the same TV shows.

    I would _____

    Why? _____

What to Do Now

You need to think ahead to predict a possible problem. Then, you can choose the best way to prevent that problem.

Read each situation below. Then, write a problem that could happen and tell how you could prevent the problem.

1. Your desk is in the back of the classroom. You can't read what's written on the chalkboard.

   Possible problem: _____

   Way to prevent: _____

2. You're on a date and realize you left your money at home.

   Possible problem: _____

   Way to prevent: _____

3. You called your boss's home to tell him you wouldn't be at work that day because you're sick. Your boss's wife took the message, but forgot to give it to him.

   Possible problem: _____

   Way to prevent: _____

4. The student sitting behind you in English class teases you during class.

   Possible problem: _____

   Way to prevent: _____

5. You earned a place on the school's basketball team, but your friend didn't.

   Possible problem: _____

   Way to prevent: _____

6. You're working tonight until 9:00. Your parents expect you home by 9:15. Your boss wants you to work an extra hour.

   Possible problem: _____

   Way to prevent: _____

Did It Work?

What ways have you tried to prevent problems?   Did these ways work?

Read each way to prevent a problem.   Then, describe a situation in which you or someone you know has tried this way.   Circle **Yes** or **No** to tell whether or not it worked.

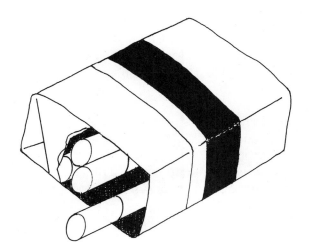

Example:

Way to prevent: Walk away.

Situation: *A friend wanted me to smoke a cigarette with her.* _____

Did it work? No

1. Way to prevent: Explain more about the situation.

   Situation: _____

   _____

   Did it work?   Yes   No

2. Way to prevent: Get help from someone before a problem happens or gets worse.

   Situation: _____

   _____

   Did it work?   Yes   No

3. Way to prevent: Don't make a big deal out of it.

   Situation: _____

   _____

   Did it work?   Yes   No

4. Way to prevent: Stay away from a person or problem situation.

   Situation: _____

   _____

   Did it work?   Yes   No

Choosing Methods of Prevention

ADDITIONAL ACTIVITIES

Your students need practice in generating acceptable ways to prevent a problem and in choosing the best method of prevention. You can continue to help them realize that preventing a problem before it occurs is usually easier than having to solve the problem. Use the activities below to help your students choose appropriate ways to prevent problems.

❑ Divide the students into small groups. Ask each group to write down two situations. One situation should describe how a student successfully prevented a problem. The other should tell of a time a student tried to prevent a problem but was not successful. The group can then think of alternative ways that may have succeeded in preventing the problem.

Discuss the situations as a class. Give praise for good ideas. Help the students be aware that sometimes good ideas don't work, but there are alternative methods.

❑ Conduct a role-playing activity called *Think Fast*. Write possible problem situations on several note cards. Have one student role-play the situation on the card. Have another student think fast to devise a method to prevent a possible problem. The first student can choose to make the problem appear or to allow the prevention of the problem. Follow each role-playing sequence with class discussion concerning the effectiveness of the prevention method used.

❑ Ask students to give examples of characters on television, in movies, or in books who are skilled at preventing problems. Discuss the methods these characters use. Have your students try to determine if these methods could work for them.

PULLING IT ALL TOGETHER

> Goal: To review and apply the steps of problem solving.

OBJECTIVES

REVIEWING THE STEPS: To review the steps in problem solving.

USING THE STEPS: To apply the steps in problem solving to realistic situations.

This section of *Problem Solving for Teens* contains exercises for your students to practice pulling together all the steps of problem solving. They'll review the steps of problem solving and then apply the process to real-life problem situations.

TEACHING SUGGESTIONS

1. Review the steps of problem solving with your whole class by asking the following questions:

    How do you recognize a serious problem?

    What are your choices for solving the problem?

    What would be your best choice of a solution?

    What would your plan of action be?

    What would be the results of this plan?

    How could you prevent a similar problem in the future?

    Provide problem situations for your students, or have them think of their own. Work through the problem situations as a class by having your students brainstorm answers to the above questions. Have someone write the important information on the chalkboard as the class discusses each question. Then, encourage your students to evaluate their ideas.

2. Have your students practice solving problems in groups of two or three people. Each group should have someone ask the leading questions, like the ones listed above, and someone write the ideas as they are discussed. Encourage every group member to participate.

    Begin by having all groups work on the same problem. Have the groups compare their results. Then, let your students solve real or fictitious problems they suggest. Later, ask your students to assess the advantages and disadvantages of working in small groups.

3. Eventually, ask your students to complete the problem solving process on their own. First, offer a fairly simple, concrete problem. Help your students think through the steps by providing examples and suggestions. Allow them to ask questions. Then, provide more difficult situations as your students improve their skills.

4. To help your students generalize the process, ask them to try problem solving outside of the classroom. Discuss the difficulties and successes they experience. Help them generate alternative solution plans if needed.

What Should I Do?

Learning to use all the steps of problem solving takes practice.

Read the problem solving information below. Then, write the letter of the step described in the blank before it. You can use a step more than once. The first one is done for you.

Problem:	Your dad asked you to mow the lawn today, but you haven't done it. You want to go to a movie with a friend in 30 minutes.

Problem solving information   *Steps*

_a___ I don't have time to mow the lawn before I go to the movie.   a. problem

_____ Mow part of the lawn.   b. solution

_____ Call my friend and tell her I can't go to the movie.

_____ Ask my dad if I can mow the lawn tomorrow right after school.

_____ I want to go to a movie, but I haven't mowed the lawn yet.

_____ Go to the movie without saying anything to my dad.

Problem:	Your best friend's birthday is today, but you forgot to buy him a gift.

Problem solving information   *Steps*

_____ I don't have anything to give my friend for his birthday.   a. problem

_____ Wish my friend "Happy Birthday" and tell him I'll give him a gift tomorrow.   b. solution

_____ Tell my friend he's not getting a birthday gift from me this year.

_____ Give my friend a birthday card instead of a gift.

_____ I feel bad because I forgot to buy my friend a birthday gift.

129

Action!

You can take action once you've thought of some solutions.

Read each problem below. Then, write the letter of the step described in the blank before it. You can use a step more than once. The first one is done for you.

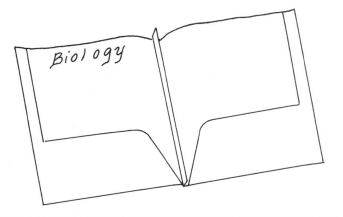

Problem:	You didn't bring home the notes you need to study for tomorrow's biology test.

Problem solving information   *Steps*

__c__   Stand at my locker and check each class's folder   a. plan of action
         to see what I need to take home.

_____   Call my friend. Go to her house. Copy her notes.   b. possible result
         Return home to study.

_____   Pass the test.   c. way to prevent

_____   During each class, write down what I need to take
         home.

_____   Fail the test.

Problem:	When you get to the checkout lane at the grocery store, you discover that you don't have enough money.

Problem solving information   *Steps*

_____   Put something back because I don't have enough   a. plan of action
         money to pay for the groceries.

_____   Check my wallet before I leave home to make sure   b. possible result
         I have enough money.

_____   I won't be able to buy the groceries I need.   c. way to prevent

_____   Put the food back. Go home and get more money.
         Return to the store and buy my groceries.

_____   I'll feel embarrassed.

Reviewing the Steps   130

Make It Right

Name _____

When you make a mistake, it's important to take care of it right away.

Read the situation below. Then, tell if the statement describes a problem or a possible solution. The first one is done for you.

Situation: While working as a waiter, you accidentally drop a customer's order on the floor as you're taking it to her.

1. Clean up the mess.   *solution* _____

2. The customer's order fell on the floor.   _____

3. Ask a co-worker to clean up the mess while you tell the customer what happened.   _____

4. Clean up the mess. Then, apologize to the customer, telling her it will be a few more minutes until her order arrives.   _____

5. Sweep the mess under the closest table and hope no one sees it. Clean up the mess later when you have time.   _____

6. The customer won't get her order right away.   _____

7. Tell the customer what happened. Explain that her order will come in a few more minutes. Offer her a free meal.   _____

8. The customer's order needs to be filled again.   _____

9. Clean up the mess when the restaurant closes.   _____

10. Ask the chef to fill the customer's order again because you dropped it.   _____

11. There's a mess on the floor which you should clean up.   _____

12. Tell your manager what happened.   _____

The Homework Assignment

Name _____

The more you practice the steps in problem solving, the easier they become.

Read the situation below. Then, decide if the statements listed after the situation describe a plan of action, a possible result, or a way to prevent the problem. The first one is done for you.

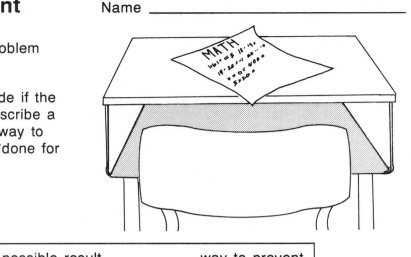

| plan of action | possible result | way to prevent |

Situation: The homework assignment you got a week ago is due today, but you don't have it done.

1. Next time, I'll finish the work earlier.   *way to prevent* _____

2. The teacher will give me some credit if I hand it in tomorrow.   _____

3. Next time, work on the assignment the same day I get it.   _____

4. Take the assignment to study hall. Ask my friends not to talk to me during study hall. Finish the assignment during study hall.   _____

5. I won't get a good grade on my assignment.   _____

6. Next time, ask a friend to remind me of the assignment two days before it's due.   _____

7. Ask the teacher if I can turn in the assignment tomorrow. Finish the assignment tonight. Turn in the assignment at 8:30 tomorrow morning.   _____

8. I'll have to work extra hard on other assignments to make up for not doing this one.   _____

9. Do as much of the assignment as I can during lunch. Hand in what I finish. Do some extra credit projects.   _____

10. Next time, work on the assignment a little at a time until it's done.   _____

11. My teacher will be disappointed with me.   _____

12. Next time, work on the assignment with a friend as soon as it's assigned.   _____

What's the Solution?

It helps to ask yourself questions as you try to solve a problem.

Read the situation below. Then, answer the questions about the problem. One question is answered for you.

Situation: You wreck your bike after a cat runs in front of you. You're not hurt, but your front bike rim is bent.

1. What is the problem?   *I can't ride my bike because the front rim is bent.*

2. Do I need to solve it right away? Why or why not? _____

_____

3. What are three possible solutions for this problem?

    a. _____

    b. _____

    c. _____

4. Which solution would work the best?

_____

Situation: You're sitting at the back of a classroom and you can't read what the teacher is writing on the chalkboard.

1. What is the problem? _____

2. Do I need to solve it right away? Why or why not? _____

_____

3. What are three possible solutions for this problem?

    a. _____

    b. _____

    c. _____

4. Which solution would work the best?

_____

133

The Wallet Discovery

Name _____

You need to ask yourself some questions before you carry out a solution plan.

Read the situation below. Then, answer the questions about the problem. Two answers are started for you.

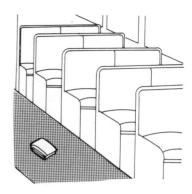

Situation: You're the only one who sees a wallet on the floor of the city bus.

1. What are the steps in my plan of action?

   a. _Pick up the wallet._ _____

   b. _____

   c. _____

2. What are two possible results of my plan?

   a. _I get a reward._ _____

   b. _____

3. What else do I need to do? _____

4. How could I prevent a similar problem? _____

   _____

Situation: You want to buy a new shirt, but you don't have enough money for it.

1. What are the steps in my plan of action?

   a. _____

   b. _____

   c. _____

2. What are two possible results of my plan?

   a. _____

   b. _____

3. What else do I need to do? _____

4. How could I prevent a similar problem? _____

   _____

Curfew Concerns

Name _____

Many problems involve your parents, your friends, and you.

Read the situation below. Then, answer the questions about the problem. One answer is started for you.

Situation: Your parents told you to be home from a party by midnight. The friend who gave you a ride isn't leaving until 1:30 A.M.

1. What is the problem? _____

_____

2. Do I need to solve it right away? Why or why not? _____

_____

3. What are three possible solutions for this problem?

    a. *Wait until my friend leaves at 1:30.* _____

    b. _____

    c. _____

4. Which solution would be the best choice? _____

5. What are the steps in my plan of action?

    a. _____

    b. _____

    c. _____

6. What are three possible results of my plan?

    a. _____

    b. _____

    c. _____

7. What else do I need to do? _____

8. How could I prevent a similar problem? _____

_____

Zip It Up

Some problems can be embarrassing, but they still need to be solved.

Read the problem below. Then, complete the problem solving steps. Two steps are started for you.

Situation: You're wearing pants and a shirt that is tucked in. Your zipper breaks during class. No one is home to bring you new pants.

1. Problem: *My pants zipper is broken.* _____

2. Possible solutions:

   a. *Ask a teacher for help.* _____

   b. _____

   c. _____

3. Best solution choice: _____

4. Plan of action:

   a. _____

   b. _____

   c. _____

   d. _____

5. Possible results:

   a. _____

   b. _____

   c. _____

6. What else do I need to do? _____

7. How could I prevent a similar problem? _____

_____

Make Everyone Happy

Name _____

Trying to please both your parents and your friends can sometimes create more problems.

Read the situation below. Then, complete the problem solving steps. One step is started for you.

Situation: Your friends come over and want you to go bowling with them. Your parents want you to wash the dishes first.

1. Problem: _____

2. Possible solutions:

    a. *Ask if I can wash the dishes later.* _____

    b. _____

    c. _____

3. Best solution choice: _____

4. Plan of action:

    a. _____

    b. _____

    c. _____

    d. _____

5. Possible results:

    a. _____

    b. _____

    c. _____

6. What else do I need to do? _____

7. How could I prevent a similar problem? _____

_____

Work Problems

Name _____

Problems often happen on the job. How you handle these problems is important to doing your job.

Read the situation below. Then, complete the problem solving steps.

Situation: Your boss schedules you to work every weekend. Another worker is scheduled to work only weeknights.

1. Problem: _____

2. Possible solutions:

    a. _____

    b. _____

    c. _____

3. Best solution choice: _____

4. Plan of action:

    a. _____

    b. _____

    c. _____

    d. _____

5. Possible results:

    a. _____

    b. _____

    c. _____

6. What else do I need to do? _____

7. How could I prevent a similar problem? _____

    _____

One Step at a Time

Name _____

Solving a problem successfully means taking one step at a time.

Think of a problem situation you or someone else has faced, and write it below. Then, complete the steps to solve the problem.

Situation: _____

_____

1. Problem: _____

2. Possible solutions:

    a. _____

    b. _____

    c. _____

3. Best solution choice: _____

4. Plan of action:

    a. _____

    b. _____

    c. _____

    d. _____

5. Possible results:

    a. _____

    b. _____

    c. _____

6. What else do I need to do? _____

7. How could I prevent a similar problem? _____

_____

Try Again

Sometimes the results of your first solution plan don't solve the problem. Then, you need to make another one and try it.

Read the problem and solution plan below. Then, make up a new solution and plan to solve the problem.

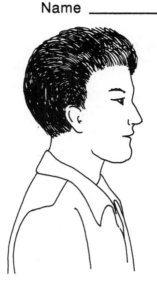

Problem: You want to ask someone for a date, but you're afraid she'll say no.

Solution: Ask a friend to go with me for support.

First plan:

    a.   My friend and I will sit near her at lunch.
    b.   We'll start talking to her.
    c.   I'll ask her for a date.

Result: My friend talked so much I never had a chance to ask her for a date.

New solution: _____

New plan:

    a. _____

    b. _____

    c. _____

Result: _____

What else do I need to do? _____

How could I prevent a similar problem in the future? _____

_____

Wise Planning

Name _____

It's always a good idea to plan ahead,
especially when solving problems.

Write down a problem you've had. Complete
the first solution and plan for the problem.
Then, make up a new solution and plan.

Problem: _____

First solution: _____

Plan of action:

    a. _____

    b. _____

    c. _____

Result: _____

Second solution: _____

Plan of action:

    a. _____

    b. _____

    c. _____

Result: _____

Did you think of both plans when you had the problem? _____

Which plan do you think is better? Why? _____

_____

The Wrong Change

Name _____

Think about all the steps you need to take to solve a problem.

Read the situation below. Then, complete each sentence to tell how you would solve the problem. The problem is identified for you.

Situation: You bought something at a store. You didn't notice until you were in the parking lot that the store clerk gave you the wrong change.

1.   The problem was that I   *didn't get the right change.* _____

2.   My choices for solutions are:

   a. _____

   b. _____

   c. _____

3.   The best choice is _____

4.   My plan of action is:

   a. _____

   b. _____

   c. _____

   d. _____

5.   After I put my plan into action, the result will probably be that _____

   _____

6.   I decided I'll also need to _____

   _____

7.   To prevent a problem like this next time, I will _____

   _____

8.   This will be a good solution because _____

   _____

Living and Learning

Name _____

When you use your problem-solving skills, you learn ways to handle future problems.

Think of a problem situation and write it below. Then, complete each sentence to tell how you would handle the situation.

Situation: _____

_____

1. The problem is that _____

_____

2. I could do one of the following:

   a. _____

   b. _____

   c. _____

3. The best solution would probably be _____

_____

4. The result would probably be that _____

_____

5. To prevent a problem like this next time, I would _____

_____

6. Solving this problem helped me learn that _____

_____

ADDITIONAL ACTIVITIES

Pulling the steps of problem solving together is a crucial skill for your students to develop. They need plenty of practice to generalize the process to real-life situations. The activities below will help your students learn how to solve problems on their own.

❑ Divide your students into pairs. Give one person a card with a problem listed on it, such as a broken item or an argument with a parent. The person with the card is the solver who verbally works through each problem solving step. The solver's partner prompts him to include all the necessary steps. Then, the partners reverse roles for the next problem.

❑ Have individual students orally practice solving typical classroom problems, like a broken pencil lead, being late to class, or having trouble with directions. While one student solves a problem, you or other students can offer cues to help. Then, give the student positive and constructive feedback.

❑ Walk with your students to various locations in the school. Discuss problems that could occur in these places. If you see a problem happening, talk through the problem-solving steps. If possible, have another teacher, a custodian, a secretary, or a cook stage problems for your students to solve as you make your journey.

❑ Take your students on field trips where they can solve real-life problems with your guidance. A trip to an obstacle course provides physical challenges that require group brainstorming to solve. A shopping center trip allows students to solve consumer problems such as how much to spend, which brand to buy, and how to locate things. At a museum, you can ask questions which lead students to different parts of the museum to obtain answers. You can also talk through general field trip problems like trouble on the bus, lunch concerns, and lost students.

❑ Ask your students to identify problems and choices for solutions from home situations. Then, review the problem-solving steps used by the students. Discuss successes, failures, and ways of preventing similar problems.

❑ Give the students weekly self-monitoring charts to record the success or failure of their problem-solving attempts. A chart is provided in the Appendix for you to reproduce as needed. Either in individual conferences or in groups, discuss what has and hasn't worked. Help your students pinpoint their strengths and weaknesses and set goals for improvement.

COMMUNICATION STRATEGIES

Goal: To communicate effectively when solving problems.

OBJECTIVES

CLARIFYING AND ELABORATING: To explain or reword ideas.

EXPRESSING CONCERNS: To explain concerns or complaints nicely in a way which results in change.

CONVINCING OR PERSUADING: To influence others to agree with you.

NEGOTIATING AND COMPROMISING: To work toward an agreement with someone.

APOLOGIZING: To tell someone you're sorry for doing something wrong.

This section of *Problem Solving for Teens* contains exercises for your students to improve their communication skills while they solve problems. The exercises will help your students learn specific ways to communicate in problem situations.

TEACHING SUGGESTIONS

1. Discuss the value of effective communication with your students. Review the problem-solving steps and encourage your students to tell why using these steps can help them communicate better.

2. Discuss ways your students can clarify and elaborate when they're communicating. Use examples to tell your students about techniques such as repeating what they've said, speaking more clearly, providing more detail, giving examples, making comparisons, drawing diagrams, and rewording things.

    Talk about these strategy steps for clarifying and elaborating:

    a. *Look* for signals of confusion from the listener.

    b. *Repeat* your idea in a clear voice.

    c. *Explain* your idea in more detail.

    d. *Reword* your idea if necessary.

3. Discuss the difference between expressing concerns in a nonproductive and productive way. It's nonproductive to complain about something without offering any suggestions. To express a concern in a productive way, you need to state a concern, tell the reason it bothers you, and offer suggestions to change the situation.

Talk about these strategy steps for expressing concerns:

    a. *State* your concern clearly in a pleasant tone of voice.

    b. *Support* your concern with reasons.

    c. *Suggest* how to make a change.

    d. *Choose* the right person, place, and time when you express your concern.

    e. *Rehearse* what to say.

4. Explain the meaning of convincing or persuading, which is influencing someone to agree with you. Discuss situations when this skill could be beneficial, such as when a student wishes to use his parents' car for the night.

    Talk about these strategy steps for convincing and persuading:

    a. *Decide* how strongly you feel.

    b. *Explain* your view clearly.

    c. *Discover* how the other person feels.

    d. *Provide* more facts, examples, and reasons.

    e. *Show* your feelings by your voice and your actions.

    Emphasize how the skills used in clarifying and expressing concerns can also be used when convincing or persuading.

5. Discuss the meaning of negotiating and compromising. Negotiating involves people listening to each other's viewpoints while they work toward an agreement. Compromising involves each person giving in a little to reach an agreement. These skills are used when the convincing process hasn't been successful.

    Talk about these strategy steps for negotiating and compromising:

    a. *Explain* your view.

    b. *Listen* to the other person's view.

    c. *Understand* the other person's view well enough to restate it.

    d. *Compromise* if you need to.

    Point out that clarifying, elaborating, convincing, and persuading are skills that can also be used when negotiating and compromising.

6. Ask your students to define *apology*. An apology is what you tell someone when you're sorry for doing something wrong. Discuss reasons for apologizing, such as to correct a problem, to make others and yourself feel better, and to begin a discussion of what went wrong.

   Talk about these strategy steps for apologizing:

   a. *Decide* if you need to apologize.

   b. *Choose* whether to say, write, or do something to apologize.

   c. *Apologize* soon in a private place.

   d. *Suggest* a way to make it up to the person.

Watch for Signals

Watch for signals from your listeners to see if they understand what you're saying.

Read each statement below. If the statement shows that the listener understands, write **Yes** in the blank in front of that statement. If the statement shows that the listener doesn't understand, write **No** in the blank. The first one is done for you.

_No_   1. The listener scratches his head.

_____ 2. The listener asks, "What did you say?"

_____ 3. The listener nods her head.

_____ 4. The listener smiles.

_____ 5. The listener says, "Huh?"

_____ 6. The listener says, "I understand."

_____ 7. The listener asks, "Could you say that again?"

_____ 8. The listener claps her hands.

_____ 9. The listener makes no response.

_____ 10. The listener says, "I don't get it."

_____ 11. The listener gives you a *thumbs up* sign.

_____ 12. The listener asks you to repeat what you said.

_____ 13. The listener shakes his head.

_____ 14. The listener has a questioning look in her eyes.

_____ 15. The listener says, "I agree with you."

_____ 16. The listener frowns.

Tell It All

If your listener is confused, you may need to add more details to what you said, or give some examples.

Read each problem and statement below. Then, give more information to make the statement clearer.

Example:

Problem: You dropped your tray of food on the cafeteria floor.

Your statement: "Everyone looked at me. I felt dumb."

Additional information: *I dropped my lunch tray in the cafeteria and everyone stared at me.*

1. Problem: You lost your math book.

    Your statement: "It was gone when I went back to my desk."

    Additional information: _____

    _____

2. Problem: You can't find the right house for a pizza delivery.

    Your statement: "Where do I take this pizza?"

    Additional information: _____

    _____

3. Problem: You need to provide popcorn for an art project.

    Your statement: "Dad, I need to take some popcorn to school."

    Additional information: _____

    _____

4. Problem: You want your friend to go downtown with you.

    Your statement: "Will you go with me?"

    Additional information: _____

    _____

149

Reword Your Idea

Sometimes you need to reword something you've said so your listener can understand you better. You need to give the same information, but with different words.

Read each problem and statement below. Then, reword the statement so it's clearer.

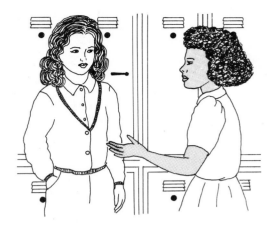

Example:

Problem: Your friend has been spreading rumors about you.

Your statement: "Please don't tell stories about me that aren't true."

Rewording: *I feel bad when you tell lies about me.* _____

1. Problem: You can't remember all your duties at work.

   Your statement: "Mr. Hanks, tell me what I should do."

   Rewording: _____

   _____

2. Problem: You can't get your math homework because your locker door won't open.

   Your statement: "I can't get my homework out of my locker, Ms. Kline."

   Rewording: _____

   _____

3. Problem: Your brother talks to you while you're trying to study.

   Your statement: "Leave me alone!"

   Rewording: _____

   _____

4. Problem: You have to leave a message on your friend's answering machine.

   Your statement: "This is Carl. Call me soon."

   Rewording: _____

   _____

150

Make It Clear

You need to explain your problems clearly so your listeners can understand them.

Read each problem and statement. Then, make each statement clearer by answering the questions.

Problem: Your dog is lost.

Your statement: "The pen was empty when I got home from school."

1. Tell two ways your listener might signal his confusion.

    a. _____

    b. _____

2. Add these details to your statement:

    a. What kind of pen was empty? _____

    b. What does your dog look like? _____

    c. When did you last see your dog? _____

3. How could you reword your first statement? _____

    _____

Problem: You broke your ankle while you were hiking.

Your statement: "I tripped on something."

1. Tell two ways your listener might signal her confusion.

    a. _____

    b. _____

2. Add these details to your statement:

    a. What did you trip on? _____

    b. Where were you when you tripped? _____

    c. How badly were you hurt? _____

3. How could you reword your first statement?

    _____

ADDITIONAL ACTIVITIES

For successful communication, your students need to recognize when their listeners are confused and then modify their messages. Use the activities below to help your students communicate more effectively.

❑ Choose one student to be a speaker. Give him a diagram, map, or picture to describe to the class without showing it to them. Encourage the speaker to look for signals from his listeners telling him whether or not they understand what he's saying. When the listeners appear confused, the speaker should repeat, clarify, or reword his message as needed. Have the students take turns being the speaker.

❑ Have your students practice clarifying statements as they work through the problem-solving process. Have six students complete the following steps:

Provide the first student with an unclear statement of a problem, such as "I don't know how to get to their house." Have the student read the statement to the class and look for signals of confusion from the class. Then, encourage her to add more details to make the statement clearer.

The second student's task is to think of three possible solutions for the problem. Encourage him to look for signals of confusion from the class, add details and examples, or reword his ideas.

Have the third student choose the solution she thinks is the best and state it clearly. Then, ask her to repeat her choice.

Encourage the fourth student to develop a plan of action. He can use diagrams, examples, or comparisons to communicate his plan effectively.

Have the fifth student list three possible results of the plan, clarifying anything that may be unclear.

Finally, have the last student tell how a similar problem could be prevented. Then, have her reword her statement.

State Your Concern

Name _____

When you express a concern, you need to state it clearly.

Read each situation below. Then, state a concern you might have in that situation. The first one is done for you.

1. Situation: The new radio you bought doesn't work right.

    Concern: *I can't pull up the antenna very far.* _____

2. Situation: Your watch isn't running right.

    Concern: _____

3. Situation: You have a lot of homework.

    Concern: _____

4. Situation: Your parents are old-fashioned.

    Concern: _____

5. Situation: An older student is bothering you at school.

    Concern: _____

6. Situation: You don't like your work schedule.

    Concern: _____

7. Situation: Your neighbor's dog bothers you.

    Concern: _____

8. Situation: You aren't happy with your English grade.

    Concern: _____

9. Situation: Your friend owes you money.

    Concern: _____

10. Situation: Your allowance is too small.

    Concern: _____

Support and Suggest

Support your concerns with reasons and then suggest how to make some changes.

Read each concern below. First, give a reason for the concern. Then, suggest a change. One reason and suggestion are done for you.

1. Concern: The large stacks of newspapers in the basement need to be moved.

   Reason: *They can be a fire hazard.* _____

   Suggestion: *Bundle the newspapers and take them to a recycling center.* _____

2. Concern: You just turned 16 and you want a later weekend curfew.

   Reason: _____

   Suggestion: _____

3. Concern: After two years at your job, you want a raise.

   Reason: _____

   Suggestion: _____

4. Concern: You don't like what your dad is fixing for supper.

   Reason: _____

   Suggestion: _____

5. Concern: You don't want to watch the videotape your friend chose.

   Reason: _____

   Suggestion: _____

6. Concern: You like to sing in the choir, but you don't want to sing a solo.

   Reason: _____

   Suggestion: _____

7. Concern: You didn't have enough time to finish your history test.

   Reason: _____

   Suggestion: _____

Who? When? Where?

Name _____

When you need to express a concern, talk to the person who can do something to change the situation.

Read each situation below. Then, state the concern and answer the questions. The first one is done for you.

Example:

Situation: You receive several prank phone calls while you're home alone.

    a. Concern: _I want the prank phone calls to stop._

    b. Who to talk to: _the police_

    c. When? _right away_

    d. Where? _Call the police station from home._

1. Situation: You asked the beautician to dye your hair blond, but the color looks greenish.

    a. Concern: _____

    b. Who to talk to: _____

    c. When? _____

    d. Where? _____

2. Situation: Water dripping from the ceiling has made the bed wet in your motel room.

    a. Concern: _____

    b. Who to talk to: _____

    c. When? _____

    d. Where? _____

3. Situation: You got a different kind of pizza than you ordered.

    a. Concern: _____

    b. Who to talk to: _____

    c. When? _____

    d. Where? _____

Practice Makes Perfect

Practice what you'll say when you express your concern. You can practice alone or with someone.

Read each situation below. Then, complete the information you'll need to practice expressing your concern. The first one is started for you.

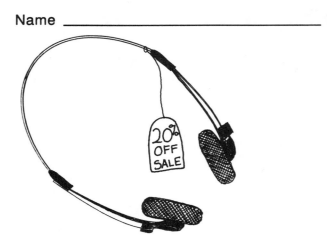

1. Situation: You bought some headphones that were on sale, but the clerk charged you the regular price.

    a. Concern: *I want some money back from the clerk.* _____

    b. Reason: *I paid the regular price instead of the sale price.* _____

    c. Suggestion: _____

    d. Who to talk to: _____

    e. When? _____

    f. Where? _____

2. Situation: You were laid off from your job, even though you had worked there longer than someone who wasn't laid off.

    a. Concern: _____

    b. Reason: _____

    c. Suggestion: _____

    d. Who to talk to: _____

    e. When? _____

    f. Where? _____

3. Situation: Your sisters are making a lot of noise while you're studying.

    a. Concern: _____

    b. Reason: _____

    c. Suggestion: _____

    d. Who to talk to: _____

    e. When? _____

    f. Where? _____

156

ADDITIONAL ACTIVITIES

Expressing concerns in a productive way lets your students complain in a way that facilitates change. By explaining the reason for the concern and offering suggestions, your students are more likely to get the results they desire. The activities below will help your students express their concerns in an effective and carefully planned way.

❑ Ask your students to describe situations that could result in concerns or complaints. Then, divide your students into groups of five. Next, use a situation that was described to do the following activity. The first person states the concern clearly in a pleasant tone of voice. The second person supports the concern with a reason. The third person suggests how to make productive changes. The fourth person chooses the right person, time, and place to express the concern. The fifth person combines everyone's input, rehearses the concern, and presents it. Finally, group members give each other feedback.

❑ Have the students work in groups of three to present concerns to the class in the following manner. One person states the concern. Another person supports the concern with a reason. The third person suggests how to make a change. Then, the rest of the class decides whether or not the concern was expressed in a productive way.

❑ Have each student prepare a concern and present it. Ask each student to describe the process he used to prepare the concern and to demonstrate his rehearsal. Encourage each student to decide whether or not his concern was expressed in a productive way. If a concern wasn't expressed in a productive way, have students help each other by offering suggestions for how to express it more productively.

Decide How You Feel

The first step in convincing someone is to decide how strongly you feel about something.

Read each topic below. Then, circle **1**, **2**, or **3** to show how strongly you feel about the topic. Circle **Yes** or **No** to tell if you think you could convince someone to agree with you. If you circle **Yes**, tell who you'd convince.

```
1 = no real opinion
2 = somewhat positive or negative feeling
3 = strong positive or negative feeling
```

Example:

Recycling aluminum cans   1   2   3

  a. Could you convince someone to agree with you?   (Yes)   No

  b. If yes, who?   *my parents* _____

1. No homework on weekends   1   2   3

  a. Could you convince someone to agree with you?   Yes   No

  b. If yes, who? _____

2. No drinking and driving   1   2   3

  a. Could you convince someone to agree with you?   Yes   No

  b. If yes, who? _____

3. Wanting to go to a friend's party   1   2   3

  a. Could you convince someone to agree with you?   Yes   No

  b. If yes, who? _____

4. Saying no to drugs   1   2   3

  a. Could you convince someone to agree with you?   Yes   No

  b. If yes, who? _____

5. Wanting a school dance   1   2   3

  a. Could you convince someone to agree with you?   Yes   No

  b. If yes, who? _____

Explain Your View

To convince another person, you need to explain your view clearly and support it with facts, examples, or reasons.

Read each view below. Then, give two facts, examples, or reasons which support that view. The first one is done for you.

1. You want to try out for the basketball team.

   a. *I'm a fast runner.* _____

   b. *I practiced shooting baskets all summer.* _____

2. You want someone to work for you Saturday.

   a. _____

   b. _____

3. You want a telephone in your bedroom.

   a. _____

   b. _____

4. You want to take special art lessons.

   a. _____

   b. _____

5. You want a puppy for a pet.

   a. _____

   b. _____

6. You want an extra day to finish your science report.

   a. _____

   b. _____

7. You want to leave work 30 minutes early.

   a. _____

   b. _____

Be Convincing

If you need to convince your parents to trust you, think about ways you have convinced them before.

Read the situation below. Then, complete the statements to tell how you would convince your parents.

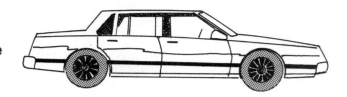

Situation:	You want to use the car Friday night. Your parents don't need the car that night, but they don't trust you with the car.

1. You feel strongly about wanting to use the car. Explain your view clearly.

   _____

   _____

2. What facts or reasons support your view?

   a. _____

   b. _____

3. How do your parents feel? _____

   _____

4. What facts or reasons support your parents' view?

   a. _____

   b. _____

5. What are some past examples you could use to convince your parents to let you use the car?

   a. _____

   b. _____

6. What kind of voice would you use? _____

7. How could you use your arms or face to show how strongly you feel? _____

   _____

8. What would you do if your parents weren't convinced? _____

   _____

ADDITIONAL ACTIVITIES

The ability to convince or persuade people can be a powerful skill for your students to use when they solve problems. Use the activities below to help your students clearly state and support their views.

❑ Examine how advertisers convince customers to buy their products by asking students to find magazine and newspaper ads and to watch television commercials. Discuss the various techniques advertisers use, such as endorsements by celebrities, testimonials, promises of a better life, and new and improved products. Have the students discuss which techniques they think are most effective.

❑ Ask each student to prepare and present a commercial for an original product. Encourage the students to be creative when they make their commercials by drawing or making the product and by using different advertising techniques.

❑ Discuss situations in which a strong tone of voice, facial expressions, or other actions play a large role in the convincing process. Show how a teacher might use these methods to convince students to be quiet, to work, or to walk in the halls.

❑ Discuss public figures like politicians who frequently use convincing skills in their communications. Talk about how they convince people to agree with them, including both what they say and how they present their message.

❑ Have pairs of students role-play situations that would require convincing someone. For example, they could act as a parent and babysitter at a house or a manager and clerk at a grocery store. Discuss the convincing techniques used, how well they worked, and how to make improvements.

Listen to Others

After you explain your view, you need to listen to find out what the other person thinks.

Read each view below. Then, write how the other person's view might be different. The first one is done for you.

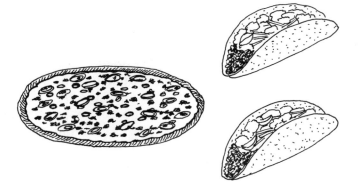

1. Your view: You want to go out for pizza.

    Your friend's view: _She's hungry for tacos._ _____

2. Your view: You want to write a one-page report.

    Your teacher's view: _____

3. Your view: You want your parents to buy a convertible.

    Your parents' view: _____

4. Your view: You think you need an hour break at work.

    Your boss's view: _____

5. Your view: You think your sister should wash the dishes.

    Your sister's view: _____

6. Your view: You want to sleep until noon on Saturdays.

    Your parents' view: _____

7. Your view: You want to go steady with the person you've been dating.

    Your date's view: _____

8. Your view: You want to chew gum in class.

    Your teacher's view: _____

9. Your view: You want to wait on tables at work, but you don't want to clean them.

    Another worker's view: _____

10. Your view: You want to talk with your friends during study hall.

    The study hall supervisor's view: _____

Try to Understand

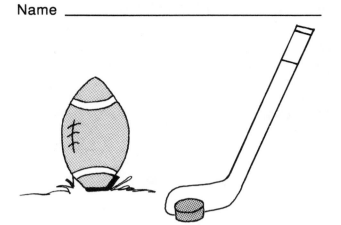

If you can't agree with someone, suggest a compromise.

Read each situation below. Then, write a question which could help you understand the other person's point of view. Finally, write a possible compromise. The first one is done for you.

1. Situation: You want your friend to go to a hockey game with you. Your friend doesn't like hockey.

    Question: *What part of hockey don't you like?*

    Compromise: *I'll go to a football game with you if you'll go to a hockey game with me.*

2. Situation: You want to spend the night at a friend's house. Your dad wants you to stay home with your younger brother.

    Question: _____

    Compromise: _____

    _____

3. Situation: Your boss wants you to come to work at 6:00 A.M. You don't want to come in until 7:30.

    Question: _____

    Compromise: _____

    _____

4. Situation: The track coach wants you to run the mile race. You want to throw the shot put.

    Question: _____

    Compromise: _____

    _____

5. Situation: Your parents want you to try to make the honor roll at school. You just want to get passing grades.

    Question: _____

    Compromise: _____

    _____

Making a Compromise

Name _____

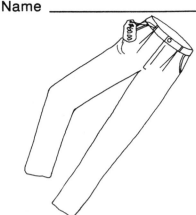

When you compromise with someone, you each give up something in order to reach an agreement.

Read each situation below. Then, suggest a compromise. The first one is done for you.

1. Situation: You want a pair of jeans which costs $60. Your parents don't want to pay that much for jeans.

    Compromise: *We each pay half the cost of the jeans.* _____

2. Situation: You want to work on weeknights only. Your boss wants you to work on weekends, too.

    Compromise: _____
    _____

3. Situation: You want to borrow your brother's cassette tape. He says you can't because you either ruin or don't return his things.

    Compromise: _____
    _____

4. Situation: You want to go see a certain movie, but your date wants to see a different one.

    Compromise: _____
    _____

5. Situation: You want to buy a stereo. Your parents want you to save your money for college.

    Compromise: _____
    _____

6. Situation: You want to ride in a friend's car to school. Your parents want you to ride the bus.

    Compromise: _____
    _____

7. Situation: You like to go right home after work. You carpool with someone who likes to go shopping after work.

    Compromise: _____
    _____

ADDITIONAL ACTIVITIES

As your students learn how to negotiate, they'll learn to try to reach agreements after explaining their views and listening to others' views. They'll find that they sometimes need to make compromises in their negotiations. The activities below will help your students learn how to negotiate and compromise more effectively.

- ❑ Describe real-life situations in which negotiating and compromising are needed, such as making laws, buying a house, making family rules, accepting a new job, and deciding how to spend your family vacation. Ask students to think of situations they're familiar with and how they reached agreements.

- ❑ Have pairs of students role-play situations that involve negotiating and compromising. For example, students can role-play a parent and a child, a teacher and a student, or a boss and an employee. Then, ask the students to switch roles, role-play the situation again, and discuss how playing each role felt. As a variation, ask the students to role-play the situation once with the characters in good moods and once with the characters in bad moods. Then, have them compare the two situations.

- ❑ Ask two pairs of students to work together. Give the students a situation that requires negotiation. Have one pair work through the negotiations while the other pair gives them prompts. Then, have the students discuss the value of using more people's ideas when trying to reach an agreement.

- ❑ Discuss the differences between arguing and negotiating. People who are arguing use an unpleasant tone of voice and don't try to understand each other's views. Ask pairs of students to make up situations that call for negotiation. Have them role-play the situations as arguments and then as negotiations. Then, have them discuss how and why the communication and results were different.

When to Apologize

When you hurt someone's feelings or you do something wrong, you need to apologize.

Read each situation below. Then, circle **Yes** or **No** to tell whether or not you need to apologize.

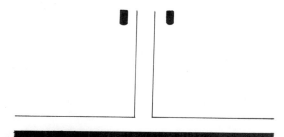

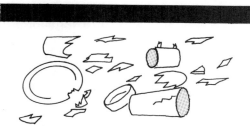

1. You accidentally broke some dishes at work.

    Do you need to apologize?   Yes   No

2. Your car was hit by a truck that went through a red light.

    Do you need to apologize?   Yes   No

3. You lost the necklace you borrowed from your mother.

    Do you need to apologize?   Yes   No

4. You stepped on someone's foot in the hallway.

    Do you need to apologize?   Yes   No

5. You stepped on your friend's toes.

    Do you need to apologize?   Yes   No

6. You made a good dinner for your family.

    Do you need to apologize?   Yes   No

7. You spilled food on a customer at work.

    Do you need to apologize?   Yes   No

8. You lied to your friend and she found out.

    Do you need to apologize?   Yes   No

9. You did all your homework on time.

    Do you need to apologize?   Yes   No

10. You forgot to give your dad a telephone message.

    Do you need to apologize?   Yes   No

Ways to Apologize

Name _____

Think of all the ways you could apologize to someone.

Read each situation below. Then, tell what you could say, write, and do to apologize in each situation. The first one is done for you.

1. You forgot your friend's birthday.

   Say it: _*I'm sorry I forgot your birthday.*_____

   Write it: _*Send a belated birthday card with your written apology.*_____

   Do it: _*Give her a gift.*_____

2. Your sister waited outside the school for an hour because you forgot to pick her up.

   Say it: _____

   Write it: _____

   Do it: _____

3. You told an embarrassing secret about your friend.

   Say it: _____

   Write it: _____

   Do it: _____

4. You were late for work because you talked too long on the phone.

   Say it: _____

   Write it: _____

   Do it: _____

5. You broke your teacher's coffee mug.

   Say it: _____

   Write it: _____

   Do it: _____

Make an Apology

You can say, write, or do something to make an apology.

Read each situation below. Then, tell what you could say, write, and do to apologize in each situation.

1. You said something mean to your sister.

    Say it: _____

    Write it: _____

    Do it: _____

2. You gave a customer the wrong change.

    Say it: _____

    Write it: _____

    Do it: _____

3. You forgot to go to play practice after school.

    Say it: _____

    Write it: _____

    Do it: _____

4. You borrowed a friend's book without asking him.

    Say it: _____

    Write it: _____

    Do it: _____

Now, make up a situation where you need to make an apology. Then, tell the different ways you could make the apology.

5. Situation: _____

    Say it: _____

    Write it: _____

    Do it: _____

168

Planning an Apology

Name _____

Before you make an apology, you need to carefully plan what you will say and do.

Read the situation below. Then, answer each question about your apology plan.

Situation: Your friend Sue drives the family car to school. You share a locker with Sue and decide to take the keys and go out for lunch. You scrape the side of the car while you're parking it. You know Sue's parents won't let her use the car again.

1. Why do you need to apologize? _____

2. What are three ways you could apologize?

    a. _____

    b. _____

    c. _____

3. Which way do you think would work best? Why? _____

_____

4. When would you apologize? _____

5. Where would you apologize? _____

6. What way could you suggest to make it up to Sue? _____

_____

7. What are three possible results of your plan?

    a. _____

    b. _____

    c. _____

8. How could you prevent a similar problem in the future? _____

_____

ADDITIONAL ACTIVITIES

When your students make mistakes, they need to know how to apologize. Use the activities below to help your students make well planned apologies.

- ❑ Divide the class into three groups. Describe a situation in which someone needs to apologize. Have each group role-play a different method of apology, either spoken, written, or shown. Have each group also tell where and when the apology should be made. Then, as a large group, decide which method of apology would be the best choice and discuss why.

- ❑ Ask students to describe apologies they have seen on television, in movies, or in books. Discuss whether each apology seems genuine or insincere. Talk about how to determine if an apology is sincere and the negative effects of apologies that aren't sincere.

- ❑ Describe a situation in which an apology is needed. Choose one student to stand in the hallway while someone in the room makes an appropriate apology. Then, have the student in the hallway return to the room and share his method of apologizing for the same situation. Have the students compare the two apologies.

APPENDIX A

Name _____

Use this worksheet to review Unit 1: Problems. If you don't know or remember how to complete a question, refer to the worksheets you did in Unit 1.

1. Situation: _____

   _____

2. What's the problem? _____

   _____

3. Is the problem easy to fix or hard to fix? Explain your answer.

   _____

   _____

4. Should the problem be solved now, soon, or later? Explain your answer.

   _____

   _____

5. What are some clues that could have signaled a possible problem?

   _____

   _____

6. Who should be responsible for solving the problem? Why? _____

   _____

7. Could someone help solve the problem? Who? _____

   _____

8. How could that person help solve the problem? _____

   _____

Name _____

Use this worksheet to review Unit 2: Choices. If you don't know or remember how to complete a question, refer to the worksheets you did in Unit 2.

1. Problem: _____

   _____

2. Possible solutions:

   a. _____

   b. _____

   c. _____

3. Guess how much time, energy, and money it will take to use each solution.

   a. Time _____   Energy _____   Money _____

   b. Time _____   Energy _____   Money _____

   c. Time _____   Energy _____   Money _____

4. What are some pros and cons of each solution?

   a. Pros _____

      Cons _____

   b. Pros _____

      Cons _____

   c. Pros _____

      Cons _____

5. What resources do you need for this problem?

   a. _____

   b. _____

   c. _____

6. What resources do you already have?

   a. _____

   b. _____

   c. _____

7. Which is your best solution? Explain your answer. _____

   _____

Use this worksheet to review Unit 3: Plans. If you don't know or remember how to complete a question, refer to the worksheets you did in Unit 3.

1. Problem: _____

_____

2. Solution: _____

_____

3. Steps in your solution plan:

_____ a. _____

_____ b. _____

_____ c. _____

_____ d. _____

_____ e. _____

4. What order should you follow in your plan? Write a **1** on the blank in front of the first step, a **2** by the second step, and so on.

5. What questions could you ask to check your planning? _____

_____

_____

6. When would you take your first step? _____

7. Will the problem be solved after you follow all the steps? Yes No

8. What materials or tools do you need to solve the problem? _____

_____

9. Which materials would you need to get? _____

_____

10. Who could help you solve the problem? _____

11. How would you contact that person? _____

12. How might your parents react to the problem? _____

_____

Use this worksheet to review Unit 4: Results. If you don't know or remember how to complete a question, refer to the worksheets you did in Unit 4.

1. Problem: _____

    _____

2. Solution: _____

    _____

3. When is the best time to talk to other people involved in the problem?

    _____

4. Possible solution plans:

    a. _____

    b. _____

    c. _____

5. Possible outcomes:

    a. _____

    b. _____

    c. _____

6. Who caused the problem? _____

7. How can you check the results of your plan? _____

    _____

8. What could you learn from the situation? _____

    _____

9. What would be a good reward for solving the problem? _____

    _____

Unit 4 Review Sheet   174

Use this worksheet to review Unit 5: Preventing Problems. If you don't know or remember how to complete a question, refer to the worksheets you did in Unit 5.

1. Problem: _____

    _____

2. What are some early signs that may have pointed to this problem? _____

    _____

3. How could the problem have been prevented? _____

    _____

4. Put a check mark in front of each thing you could have saved by preventing the problem.

    _____ Time   _____ Energy   _____ Money

5. List another benefit of preventing this problem. _____

    _____

6. Tell about a past problem that might help you know what to do for this problem.

    _____

    _____

7. What could you learn from solving this problem? _____

    _____

8. How could you prevent a similar problem in the future? _____

    _____

Use this worksheet to review Unit 6: Pulling It All Together. If you don't know or remember how to complete a question, refer to the worksheets you did in Unit 6.

1. Situation: _____

_____

2. What's the problem? _____

3. Do I need to solve it right away? Why or why not? _____

_____

4. What are three possible solutions for this problem?

    a. _____

    b. _____

    c. _____

5. Which solution would work the best? Why? _____

_____

6. What are the steps in my plan of action?

    a. _____

    b. _____

    c. _____

7. What are two possible results of my plan?

    a. _____

    b. _____

8. What else do I need to do? _____

_____

9. How could I prevent a similar problem? _____

_____

10. Solving this problem helped me learn that _____

_____

Use this worksheet to review Unit 7: Communication Strategies. If you don't know or remember how to complete a question, refer to the worksheets you did in Unit 7.

1. Problem situation: _____

2. Your concern: _____

3. Who would you talk to about your concern? _____

4. When and where would you talk to the person? _____

5. How could you use your arms or face to show how strongly you feel? _____

   _____

6. How might your listener signal that he was confused by your statement?

   _____

7. How could you reword your statement if your listener was confused? _____

   _____

8. What changes would you suggest to fix the problem? _____

   _____

9. What facts or reasons support your view?

   a. _____

   b. _____

10. What are some past examples you could use to convince your listener to agree with you?

    a. _____

    b. _____

11. What would you do if your listener wasn't convinced? _____

    _____

12. What compromise could you make? _____

    _____

13. Do you need to apologize?   Why or why not? _____

    _____

14. How would you apologize? _____

APPENDIX B

Use this chart to keep track of how you solve your problems. For each day, write down your problems and solutions. Then, put a check mark in the Worked or Didn't Work column to tell the results of each solution.

	Problems	Solutions	Worked	Didn't Work
Sun				
Mon				
Tue				
Wed				
Thu				
Fri				
Sat				

Self-Monitoring Chart

APPENDIX C

Here is a list of typical problems encountered by teenagers. Use these pages as a reference to make up problem situations for your students to solve either on some of the worksheets or in a class or group discussion. Feel free to add other problems to the list and encourage your students to think of problem situations they're familiar with.

1. You lost your house key.

2. Your watch broke.

3. You forgot your gym clothes at home.

4. You have no lunch money.

5. Your bicycle has a flat tire.

6. You fight with your sister about which TV show to watch.

7. You forget your pencil a lot.

8. You don't like taking care of your dog.

9. You think your curfew is too early.

10. Your favorite jeans are wearing out.

11. You don't understand your homework.

12. Your friend is always late.

13. Your football team is in last place.

14. You don't like your new haircut.

15. You ran out of allowance money.

16. You can't remember your work schedule.

17. Your tape cassette player isn't working.

18. You can't find one of your shoes.

19. Your room is a mess.

20. It's very cold outside.

21. You got an *F* on a test.

22. The arcade is too far to walk to.

23. You didn't make the basketball team.

24. A drawer in your dresser is jammed shut.

25. Your mother buys you clothes you don't like. You want to tell her, but you don't want to hurt her feelings.

26. You asked someone to go to a movie with you, but you don't have any way to get there and back.

27. You want to buy a compact disc player, but it costs too much money.

28. You're working with computers in math and you don't understand how to use one. The teacher is sending home a failing notice.

29. You want to get your ears pierced, but your parents don't approve.

30. You're driving to a party alone and you're lost. The gas gauge is on empty and there's no gas station in sight.

31. You just erased a whole program on the computer by mistake.

32. Your family is going on vacation to a cabin. Your friend asked you to go with their family to Florida during the same week.

33. Your friend likes to shoplift even when you're around him. You're afraid you might get blamed for something he did.

34. You're with a friend who has been drinking and driving. He gets stopped by a police officer. Your parents will be notified.

35. You've been at a new school for two weeks, but you still have a hard time finding your way around. You're frequently late for class.

36. You really like someone at your school. You don't know how to meet and get to know him (her).

37. You only get $5 a week for allowance. You can't get a job because your parents want you to be involved in school activities. You feel like you never have enough money.

38. Your dog is getting old. He is losing his hearing and needs to take two kinds of medicine every day.

39. Your parents have strict rules about what you can wear.

40. Another employee at work is lazy and talks a lot when he works. Your boss thinks you are the one responsible for not getting things done.

41. Your friend wants you to lie to her parents, telling them she was at your house last night.

42. Some of your classmates are pressuring you to try drugs.

43. You frequently fall in gym class and the other students laugh at you.

44. You want to see an R-rated movie, but you're afraid the person at the ticket counter will ask you for your ID if you try to come in.

45. Your teacher accused you of cheating on a test, but you didn't. It's a teacher you don't like, and you're getting a *D* in her class.

46. You've been working at your job for a year. You think you deserve a raise, but you're afraid to ask your boss.

47. You had some friends over to your house while your parents were out. Your parents came home early and were upset that you didn't ask them permission to have friends over.

48. You're 25 pounds overweight. Every time you try to diet, you get upset about something and end up eating more.

49. Your parents fight all the time and you can't sleep when you hear them fighting. You're falling asleep in classes because you haven't been sleeping well at night.

50. Your dad drinks a lot and you're afraid to invite friends over to your house because of what your dad might say or do.

51. Your parents are upset because you took the family car without their permission.

52. You're afraid to talk to people you don't know.